DEFENCE OF
EUTHYPHRO,

PLATO (*c*.427–347 BC), Athenian philosopher-dramatist, has had a profound and lasting influence upon Western intellectual tradition. Born into a wealthy and prominent family, he grew up during the conflict between Athens and the Peloponnesian states which engulfed the Greek world from 431 to 404 BC. Following its turbulent aftermath, he was deeply affected by the condemnation and execution of his revered master Socrates (469–399) on charges of irreligion and corrupting the young. In revulsion from political activity, Plato devoted his life to the pursuit of philosophy and to composing memoirs of Socratic enquiry cast in dialogue form. He was strongly influenced by the Pythagorean thinkers of southern Italy and Sicily, which he is said to have visited when he was about 40. Some time after returning to Athens, he founded the Academy, an early ancestor of the modern university, devoted to philosophical and mathematical enquiry, and to the education of future rulers or 'philosopher-kings'. The Academy's most celebrated member was the young Aristotle (384–322), who studied there for the last twenty years of Plato's life. Their works mark the highest peak of philosophical achievement in antiquity, and both continue to rank among the greatest philosophers of all time.

Plato is the earliest Western philosopher from whose output complete works have been preserved. At least twenty-five of his dialogues are extant, ranging from fewer than twenty to more than 300 pages in length. For their combination of dramatic realism, poetic beauty, intellectual vitality, and emotional power they are unique in Western literature.

DAVID GALLOP is Professor of Philosophy (Emeritus) at Trent University, Ontario. He was educated at Tonbridge School and Magdalen College, Oxford. He taught philosophy at the University of Toronto (1955–69) and at Trent University (1969–89). He has also taught at Princeton University, at the University of Canterbury, New Zealand, and at the Australian National University. Besides his editions of the *Phaedo* for the Clarendon Plato and Oxford World's Classics Series, his publications include *Parmenides of Elea* (Toronto, 1984) and *Aristotle on Sleep and Dreams* (Peterborough, Ontario, 1991).

OXFORD WORLD'S CLASSICS

*For over 100 years Oxford World's Classics have brought
readers closer to the world's great literature. Now with over 700
titles—from the 4,000-year-old myths of Mesopotamia to the
twentieth century's greatest novels—the series makes available
lesser-known as well as celebrated writing.*

*The pocket-sized hardbacks of the early years contained
introductions by Virginia Woolf, T. S. Eliot, Graham Greene,
and other literary figures which enriched the experience of reading.
Today the series is recognized for its fine scholarship and
reliability in texts that span world literature, drama and poetry,
religion, philosophy and politics. Each edition includes perceptive
commentary and essential background information to meet the
changing needs of readers.*

OXFORD WORLD'S CLASSICS

═══

PLATO

Defence of Socrates
Euthyphro
Crito

═══

Translated with an Introduction and Notes by
DAVID GALLOP

OXFORD

UNIVERSITY PRESS

Great Clarendon Street, Oxford OX2 6DP

Oxford University Press is a department of the University of Oxford.
It furthers the University's objective of excellence in research, scholarship,
and education by publishing worldwide in

Oxford New York

Athens Auckland Bangkok Bogotá Buenos Aires Calcutta
Cape Town Chennai Dar es Salaam Delhi Florence Hong Kong Istanbul
Karachi Kuala Lumpur Madrid Melbourne Mexico City Mumbai
Nairobi Paris São Paulo Singapore Taipei Tokyo Toronto Warsaw

with associated companies in Berlin Ibadan

Oxford is a registered trade mark of Oxford University Press
in the UK and in certain other countries

Published in the United States
by Oxford University Press Inc., New York

Translation and editorial material © David Gallop 1997

First published as a World's Classics paperback 1997
Reissued as an Oxford World's Classics paperback 1999
Reissued 2008

British Library Cataloguing in Publication Data

Data available

Library of Congress Cataloging in Publication Data

Plato
[Dialogues. English. Selections]
Defence of Socrates; Euthyphro; Crito / Plato; translated with
an introduction and notes by David Gallop.
(Oxford world's classics)
Includes bibliographical references and indexes.
1. Socrates. I. Gallop, David. II. Title. III. Series.
B365.A5G35 1997 184—dc20 96-34134

ISBN 978-0-19-954050-1

12

Printed in Great Britain by
Clays Ltd, St Ives plc

CONTENTS

In memory of my brother

ROBIN

INTRODUCTION

THE events dramatized in Plato's *Euthyphro*, *Defence of Socrates*, and *Crito* took place in the spring of 399 BC, when Socrates was 70 and Plato probably in his late twenties. Socrates was indicted before an Athenian 'People's Court' of 500 jurors, on charges of religious innovation and corrupting the young. He was convicted and sentenced to death. After a month in prison he was executed by hemlock poisoning. The occasion was commemorated by Plato in the *Phaedo*, which forms a sequel to the present works.

Plato's writings are a testament to his master's inspiration and unique personal example. Most feature Socrates as a principal character, though in some he plays a subordinate role, and in a work of Plato's old age, the *Laws*, he has disappeared altogether. The three present works are thought by many scholars to have been composed early in Plato's career, within a decade or so of Socrates' death, while memories of the event were still fresh. They form a thematic sequence as well as a dramatic one. Each raises, from a different perspective, fundamental issues concerning the basis of moral, religious, legal, and political obligation. By dramatizing Socrates' conduct before, during, and after his trial, Plato explores these issues with a freshness and directness that have never been surpassed. For this alone, to say nothing of their literary brilliance, all three works fully deserve their status as 'classics'.

Plato's life spanned the last quarter of the fifth century and the first half of the fourth. His childhood and early youth coincided with the disastrous conflict in which Athens and her allies were pitted against Sparta and other city-states of the Peloponnese, and which embroiled the entire Greek world from 431 to 404. The events of the war and its aftermath are graphically recorded by two contemporary historians, Thucydides and Xenophon. Following Athens' humiliating defeat, her democracy was replaced by a brutal oligarchy, known as the 'Thirty Tyrants'. This conducted an eight-month reign of terror, in which 1,500 citizens are said to have been summarily executed, while thousands more fled the city. Plato's revulsion at the crimes of the Thirty, in which members of his own family were implicated, is attested in his (possibly spurious) Seventh Letter (324c–326b). The author of that document also tells us that when the democracy was restored, it initially behaved with moderation. Later, however, it shocked him by its treatment of his friend Socrates, who least of all men deserved to be charged with impiety. Eventually the author came to despair of all existing political systems. He resolved to devote himself henceforth to philosophy, which alone offered any hope for improvement of the human condition.

Plato has endowed the events of 399 with a significance which far transcends their own time and place. In many ways they now seem comparable with the trial and death of Christ. It should be remembered, however, that Plato's portrayals of them belong to the genre of literary fiction rather than biography or history. As evidence of fact, they are not necessarily to be preferred to other sources. Valuable memoirs of Socrates are also extant in Xenophon's *Memorabilia*, *Defence of Socrates*, and *Symposium*. Aristophanes' comedy the *Clouds*, first performed in 423, contains an entertaining caricature of Socrates, with much useful background for understanding the charges against him. We can also learn from occasional allusions in the treatises of Aristotle, who was born fifteen years after Socrates' death, and studied as a young man in Plato's Academy. In addition, much anecdotal material from later tradition is preserved in *The Lives of the Philosophers* by Diogenes Laertius, dating from the third century of our era.

The *Euthyphro* is cast in the simplest of all Platonic dialogue forms, a conversation between Socrates and a single interlocutor. Socrates meets Euthyphro at the Porch of the King Archon. Both have lawsuits pending. Socrates faces prosecution for impiety, while Euthyphro is prosecuting his own father on a charge of homicide. Euthyphro claims that his action is a model of piety (5d). Yet his conversation with Socrates suggests that a man charged with impiety may exemplify piety better than one who claims that virtue for himself.

This irony is so transparent as to cast doubt upon the historical reality of Euthyphro's case. An attack upon one's own father was, by ordinary Greek norms, a paradigm of impious conduct. This makes Euthyphro's initial attempt to explain piety by citing his own action seem artificial. It has been doubted, moreover, whether a crime committed on the island of Naxos (4c) could have come before an Athenian court as late as 399. Athens had lost her jurisdiction over that island when the Peloponnesian War ended in 404. If such a case ever came to court, it seems likely that Plato has juxtaposed it with the trial of Socrates, and adapted it in other ways, to suit the purposes of his philosophical fiction.

Euthyphro himself, however, like almost all other named characters in Plato's dialogues, is probably a real person. A 'Euthyphro' is mentioned several times in the *Cratylus* as an enthusiastic etymologist. The first mention of him in that work (396d) alludes to his interest in 'purification' (cf. 4b–c), and to oracular utterances he has inspired in Socrates. That fits with our dialogue's portrait of him as a 'prophet' (3c, 3e), a religious zealot of narrow and obsessive cast of mind. He is well disposed towards Socrates as a comrade in misfortune (3a–c); but his patronizing manner (3e), complacency (4b), vanity (5a, 13e), and logical ineptitude (10a, 11b, 12a, 15b) quickly establish him as a ludicrous and pathetic figure. His nearest modern counterpart would be an obtuse fundamentalist with a totally closed mind.

In justifying the prosecution of his father, Euthyphro claims to have special expertise in religious law 'about what is holy and unholy' (4e–5a). Socrates therefore asks for his help in defining 'the holy and the unholy', as we have usually translated those difficult terms. In seeking to clarify an important quality of character or conduct, the *Euthyphro* follows a pattern common to at least seven other Platonic dialogues. Like nearly all of them, it fails to reach any explicit solution. Any interpretation of such works must ask whether their failure is to be taken at face value, or whether a positive solution is somehow hidden within them. A possible answer to this question for the *Euthyphro* will emerge as we trace the course of its argument.

Five suggestions for understanding holiness are canvassed: (1) the prosecution of wrongdoers, as in Euthyphro's action against his father (5d–e); (2) whatever is agreeable to the gods (6e–7a); (3) whatever *all* the gods love (9d–e); (4) the part of justice concerned with ministering to the gods (12e, 13b); and (5) expertise in prayer and sacrifice to the gods (14b).

While each of these suggestions is rejected in turn, each failure is instructive. The first suggestion fails to recognize the difference between merely giving an example of a property and defining it. Socrates seeks a formula from which he can tell whether a particular action, such as Euthyphro's prosecution of his father, is holy or unholy (6e). Obviously, the case itself could not provide that without begging the question. But Euthyphro's answer also raises a chicken-or-egg problem. How could we ever define an ethical property except by considering particular actions, or kinds of action, which are already known to possess it, and asking what they have in common? Yet until we possess a definition, how could we know that an action like Euthyphro's has the property we are trying to define?

It may be replied that we can often know certain actions or kinds of action to possess a given property without being able to define that property. Definition is necessary only for deciding hard cases. But if so, an attempt to define an ethical property needs to begin from uncontroversial cases, and not from such highly problematic ones as Euthyphro's action. He not only fails to grasp the difference between an example and a definition, but also gives a grossly inept example. As already noted, by ordinary Greek moral norms, his action would appear to exemplify the very opposite of holiness. Even by the norms of our own age, it would be morally controversial. In addition, this first failure illustrates the difficulty of sharing an ethical inquiry with someone whose moral convictions are eccentric. With such an interlocutor, no attempt to agree upon a definition of any ethical term is likely to succeed.

We can also learn from the second failure. The formula 'what is agreeable to the gods' does not help us to decide whether a given action is holy or unholy. For both it and its opposite, 'what is disagreeable to the gods', would apply equally to one and the same action, depending on which god's response to it is invoked. Yet an adequate definition of a property requires that any instance of it should satisfy the defining formula, and not also satisfy the exact opposite of that formula. It is precisely because different parties often hold opposed attitudes to one and the same action that it is hard to define moral properties in terms of anyone's approval or disapproval. Indeed, it is to resolve such disagreements that a definition is sought.

The second definition also fails, in part, because Euthyphro accepts the theology which makes the gods differ in their loves and hates. He invokes it when he cites the violence done by Zeus and Cronus to their respective fathers, to justify his attack upon his own father (5e). Socrates neatly turns the example against him (8b), when he observes that what was pleasing to Zeus was hateful to his father, Cronus, and to his grandfather, Uranus. The traditional stories of the gods, far from setting a standard for holy conduct, provide examples of how *not* to treat one's parents. For they feature vengeful violence transmitted from one generation to the next. In making Socrates confess his distaste for such stories (6a), Plato implicitly criticizes the earliest Greek poets, Homer and Hesiod, and traditional Greek religion. He will do so again, much more explicitly, in the *Republic* (Books ii–iii).

The third definition amends the second to 'whatever *all* the gods love'. Yet it fails to explain how one could ever prove that any particular action satisfied that formula. When Socrates asks Euthyphro how he could show that all the gods approve of his prosecuting his father in the circumstances he has described, Euthyphro evades the question (9a–b). Yet the formula will be of no help, if there is no way of applying it to the circumstances of a particular case.

Waiving that difficulty (9c), however, Socrates now raises a more fundamental one. Here we enter what is perhaps the most profound, and certainly the most influential, stretch of the dialogue. Socrates asks whether the holy is holy because the gods love it, or whether they love it because it is holy (10a). Euthyphro eventually answers that the gods love what is holy *only* because it is holy (10d). It follows that its holiness cannot *consist in* their approval of it. For if it did, that same property could not also be the *ground* for their approval. The predicate 'holy' cannot therefore be equated with 'loved by all the gods'. Even if all holy actions and persons *are* loved by all the gods, their being so loved is only an attribute of them, and not the essence of their holiness (11a–b).

If that is true of 'holy', it will be equally true of other ethical predicates, such as 'right' and 'good'. Indeed, the terms in which Socrates has questioned both Euthyphro's conduct and that of his father (9a–b) show that Plato has this wider application of the point in mind. Divine approval of an action is not the essence of its rightness or goodness. There is a standard of moral behaviour independent of the divine will; and this will be true whether there be many gods or only one. The notion that religious imperatives can override the ethical norms of civilized human beings, or that divine command is the ultimate criterion for deciding what is morally right, is therefore to be rejected.

If that argument is correct, several important consequences follow. It will be mistaken to hold that a moral code requires a divine lawgiver, whose commands are enshrined in that code. Ethical standards do not derive from religious authority. Attempts to justify or to condemn a particular action morally, on the ground that it obeys or disobeys a divine law or command, are misconceived. Appeals to the divine will to prove that morally controversial types of action are right or wrong are equally misguided. Since the content of the divine will is at least as problematic as the moral issues themselves, it cannot be relied upon to settle such matters. Still more broadly, we may add, moral issues cannot be settled by appealing to the attitudes of *any* being or set of beings, whether divine or human. The point has been well expressed by a twentieth-century philosopher:

when we assert any action to be right or wrong, we are not merely making an assertion about the attitude of mind towards it of any being or set of beings whatever . . . and hence no proof to the effect that any particular being or set of beings has or has not a particular attitude of mind towards an action is sufficient to prove that the action really is right or wrong.[1]

The *Euthyphro*'s fourth definition of holiness is prefaced by the suggestion that holiness is part of the wider notion of justice or moral rectitude. On that view, holy actions are only a sub-class of just ones (12a–d). Religion is simply one department of morality, covering our duty to the gods, as distinct from our duty to our neighbour. Although this conventional view is adopted for the rest of the discussion, it seems unlikely that the reader is meant to accept it. In his *Protagoras* Plato makes Socrates argue *against* the common-sense view that holiness and justice, along with courage, temperance, and wisdom, are so many distinct 'parts' of moral excellence. Holiness is not simply 'part' of justice, but is virtually identical with it (330c–331b). On such a view, all holy actions will also be just ones, and conversely. Our duty to God is inseparable from our duty to our neighbour. In performing either sort of duty, we are performing the other.

Accepting the conventional view, however, Euthyphro and Socrates now try to specify which 'part' of justice holiness is. They consider the suggestion that it is 'ministering' to the gods. The idea that this means making the gods 'better' is rejected (13c). Euthyphro evidently assumes that gods are incapable of improvement—ironically enough, considering what his gods are like. Instead, he explains 'ministering' to the gods in terms of 'service' to them. But when asked what 'splendid task' of the gods is accomplished with the help of human service, he again dodges the question. Instead of answering it, he falls back upon the idea that holiness is expertise in prayer and sacrifice. Socrates remarks (14c) that, in refusing to specify the work of the gods, Euthyphro has turned aside just when he was on the very brink of an answer.

Many readers have felt that this is a key moment in the dialogue. Plato provides an important clue, by making Socrates say that he would have 'learnt properly' from Euthyphro about holiness, if only the latter had given the answer to which he

[1] G. E. Moore, *Ethics* (Oxford, 1912), 96.

had come so close. How, then, should Euthyphro have explicated the 'splendid task' of the gods? He might have identified it with the end that Socrates pursued in the service of his own God, the development of moral excellence in himself and others. This will be made explicit in the *Defence of Socrates*, where his calling is described as 'service' to Apollo (21e–22a, 23a–c, 30a–b). When Socrates followed that calling, by subjecting himself and others to philosophical examination, he had been practising holiness exactly as Euthyphro is now proposing to define it.

The idea of Socratic 'service to God' is also connected, as we shall shortly see, with the fate of the fifth and final attempt at definition. 'Prayer and sacrifice to the gods' entail giving them due honour and reverence, which are gratifying to them, and loved by them. But this takes us back to the third definition, which has already been discredited. The fifth definition therefore brings the conversation around in a futile circle (14c–15c).

In steering the dialogue towards this conclusion, Plato makes Socrates characterize 'expertise in prayer and sacrifice' as 'a sort of skill in mutual trading between gods and mankind' (14e). Euthyphro's grudging assent to defining holiness in such terms suggests that, like any moral quality, it goes beyond the pursuit of a good commercial bargain. In keeping with that idea, Socrates' own 'service to God' is far from being merely a 'skill in trading'. He seeks the good of others, not to gain profit for himself, but from altruistic motives, and even at personal cost. He had spoken earlier of his 'benevolence' or love of humanity (3d), a disinterested concern for the well-being of others, analogous to God's compassion for mankind. For to wish others well without getting anything in return is characteristic of the gods (15a). They have no needs which we can supply, since they alone are self-sufficient.

'Service to God' cannot, however, by itself be the solution to the problem of the *Euthyphro*. Socrates could hardly determine whether Euthyphro's action was holy or unholy by asking whether it was a service to God. For Euthyphro would doubtless have claimed that it was, and it would have been difficult to refute him. Moreover, such a definition would be open to Socrates' criticism of the third definition. As we saw, the holiness of an action does not consist in its conformity to the divine will.

But the implicit allusion to Socratic 'service to God' in the last two definitions points towards a solution. Near the end of the dialogue (15d) Socrates says, with obvious irony, that Euthyphro must surely know what the holy and unholy are. For otherwise fear of the gods and embarrassment in front of human beings would have deterred him from his present action. As things stand, however, he is sure that Euthyphro *thinks he has certain knowledge* of the holy and unholy. There could hardly be a broader hint that it is the false conceit of knowledge which has set Euthyphro upon his unholy course of action. It has stifled in him all inhibitions against unfilial conduct, leaving him stubbornly convinced that the demands of religious law can override an accepted moral norm (cf. 4e). By implication, a person who is purified of that false conceit would refrain from such conduct.

Holiness, then, is just such a purified state of mind. It is the condition which Socratic 'service to God' aims to produce: a recognition of one's own ignorance, and the quest for understanding in oneself and others. In short, the holy person is the philosopher. The 'form' or 'character' of holiness (5d, 6d) is personified by Socrates, and shown to the reader in Plato's portrait of him. Socrates himself provides the 'example' or 'standard' which he had asked for (6e). That is why he repeatedly protests his own ignorance (2c, 6b, 7a, 9a, 11d, 14d, 15c, 16a).

His protests are sometimes considered a mere pretence, in keeping with his ironic treatment of Euthyphro throughout. 'Socratic irony' is often identified with pretending not to know what one does know. But in making Socrates disclaim knowledge of holiness, Plato does not mean to depict him as insincere. Of course, Socrates does not believe that a conceited fool like Euthyphro can 'instruct' him. But his own disavowals of knowledge should be taken at face value. For he can then be seen to personify holiness in the sense suggested above: he genuinely does not know what holiness is, and he does not think that he does know. That is why the dialogue ends negatively. It aims for the same effect upon its readers as Socrates vainly tries to produce upon Euthyphro. It does not expressly tell us what holiness is, but it makes us recognize that we do not know, and provokes us into trying to find out. That is a task in which all readers of the *Euthyphro* must engage for themselves.

The *Defence of Socrates*, alone among Plato's writings, takes the form of a monologue by Socrates, which is continuous apart from a short cross-examination of his accuser, Meletus. Its traditional title, 'the *Apology*', is singularly inept: no document was ever less 'apologetic'. The Greek *apologia* means 'defence', and has been so translated here. But the work is not only, or even primarily, a defence against the specific charges on which Socrates stood trial. By setting those charges in a wider context, the *Defence of Socrates* provides a rationale for the whole Socratic way of life, and thus a defence of philosophy itself.

It is also an oratorical masterpiece. The eloquence, wit, dignity, and moral courage displayed in it can seldom have been rivalled in the history of rhetoric. But a modern reader will naturally ask about its claim to historical truth. Does the title refer to Socrates' actual defence of himself in court? Or is the work merely *a* defence of him, constructed after the event by Plato? Since Plato is twice mentioned as present at the trial (34a, 38b), it is often supposed that he remembered what Socrates had said, and recorded it for posterity as faithfully as he could. So riveting, indeed, is Socrates' address that we can almost believe ourselves in an Athenian courtroom as we read it. Even if it is not a verbatim transcript of Socrates' words, we feel that it must re-create their substance.

It is doubtful, however, whether that impression can stand up to scrutiny. The *Defence of Socrates* is, beyond question, a work of high literary art. As such, it is no more likely to be a reconstruction of Socrates' actual speech than a verbatim transcript. According to Xenophon (*Defence of Socrates* 3–9, *Memorabilia* iv. 8. 4–10), Socrates obeyed an admonition from God not to prepare a defence ahead of his trial, on the ground that it was better for him to die before the infirmities of old age set in. He therefore made no serious effort to defend himself, but resigned himself to conviction, in accordance with the will of God. Whatever we think of Xenophon's testimony, it is inconceivable that any speaker could have improvised before a real court such an artfully structured, nuanced, and polished composition as Plato's *Defence of Socrates*. That is not to say that the work falsifies any biographical facts about Socrates, still less that its content is wholly invented. For all we know to the contrary, it may even in some places faithfully reproduce what Socrates said in court. But whatever blend of fact and fiction it contains, the speech as a whole is a philosophical memoir, intended to convey a sense of Socrates' mission and the supreme injustice of his conviction. It remains, above all, an exhortation to the practice of philosophy. No less than Plato's dramatic dialogues, it is designed to draw its readers into philosophical reflection, so that they may recover for themselves the truths to which the master had borne witness.

If that is the chief aim of the *Defence*, its fidelity to fact becomes a secondary issue. As a philosophical work, its value lies in its positive statement of Socrates' message, complementing Plato's depictions of him in inconclusive works such as the *Euthyphro*. Our understanding of that dialogue is, in fact, greatly enhanced by the *Defence*. For its portrayal of Socrates provides an exemplar or model of holiness similar to that which the *Euthyphro* had suggested.

The *Defence* comprises three separate speeches: (i) Socrates' main defence (17a–35d); (ii) his proposal of a counter-penalty, following conviction (35e–38b); and (iii) his address to the jury, after sentencing (38c–42a).

The main speech has five well-marked sections: (1) a preface (17a–18a); (2) a programme for what is to follow (18a–19a); (3) a response to (*a*) the charges brought by Socrates' earlier accusers (19a–24b), and (*b*) the two specific charges in Meletus' formal indictment (24b–28a); (4) a digression (28b–34b) responding to two major objections; and (5) a conclusion, in which Socrates declines to make an emotional plea to the jury (34b–35d).

From this synopsis one might expect Socrates' response to

Meletus (24b–28a) to form the core of his defence. But if so, his answer to the indictment will seem disappointingly superficial. Meletus, nominally his chief accuser, is set up as a callow youth, incapable of standing up to a Socratic interrogation. He seems like a straw man, against whom victory is won too easily to be convincing. But that perception fails to observe Plato's strategy. Meletus' charges of atheism and religious innovation are answered superficially because they were themselves superficial, a mere front to conceal the true motives of the prosecution. Socrates has uncovered those motives in the important preceding section, where he replies to his 'earlier accusers'. Their hostility was aroused, he claims, by his philosophical mission. His quest for a rational basis for ethical beliefs had been resented by his opponents as morally subversive, and perhaps also as a threat to the restored democracy. Not only had it exposed their personal views and actions to critical scrutiny; it had also demanded a radical reordering of their values. Material wealth and worldly success would be replaced as paramount goals, both for individuals and for societies, by moral excellence.

The real reasons underlying the charges against Socrates, therefore, were to be found in his activity as a moral philosopher. In making this clear, Socrates distances himself from two sorts of thinker with whom he had been confused in the popular mind, not least by Aristophanes' good-humoured portrayal of him in the *Clouds*. In that comedy he had been caricatured as the director of a 'Thinkery', a school for intellectuals, dedicated to newfangled ideas, logical chicanery, and pseudo-science. Accordingly, in the *Defence* Socrates first disclaims any expertise or special interest in natural science (19a–d). He thus counters allegations of atheism or religious heresy: he is not an irreligious thinker of the kind often associated, in conservative opinion, with 'modern science'. As is clear from many other Platonic texts, neither Socrates nor Plato recognized the slightest conflict between science and religion. On the contrary, the *Defence* portrays Socrates as a more truly religious man than any of his accusers.

Secondly (19d–20c), Socrates distances himself from professional educators, or 'sophists', the itinerant professors who purveyed instruction in 'civic excellence' and public speaking as the key to worldly success. As the *Clouds* shows, the practice of sophists was widely associated with 'turning the weaker argument into the stronger'. The connection is still marked in our word 'sophistry' for specious argumentation. In the *Defence*, by contrast, Socrates claims only to seek the truth by honest argument. He denies that he was ever anyone's instructor (33a). He never offered to impart expertise for a fee, and he guaranteed no results. Rather, he inspired his followers to engage in a special kind of inquiry. Its effect cannot be directly transmitted from one person to another. Yet it deals, so he claimed, with matters of the utmost importance (22d). Its nature is peculiarly difficult to explain to anyone who has not been exposed to it, since it is nothing less than the quest for intellectual autonomy. Each individual must pursue it for himself or herself. Yet Plato conveys a vivid sense of it through the celebrated story of Socrates and the Delphic oracle (21a–23b). A word about this venerable institution will therefore be in order.

Delphi, situated on the southern slopes of Mount Parnassus, above the Gulf of Corinth, was the most ancient and sacred sanctuary in Greece. Its temple contained a round stone that was supposed to mark the exact centre, or 'navel', of the earth. The portals of the temple bore the inscription 'Know Thyself' and other proverbial injunctions, often cited by Plato for their ethical significance (see, especially, *Charmides* 164d–165a). Delphi was the site of the most respected and influential oracle of Greece, presided over by the god Apollo. The word for 'oracle' originally meant the response of a god to a question put to him by a worshipper. It thus came to be used for the oracular shrine itself or its priesthood. Advice from the oracle was sought, both by individuals and by states, on a wide range of personal, political, and financial matters. It was delivered either by the drawing of a lot, or through the utterance of an inspired medium, the Pythian priestess. The oracle's responses were notoriously cryptic or ambiguous. Not infrequently they required the skill of an interpreter to be correctly understood.

According to Plato's story, Chaerephon had asked the oracle

whether there was anyone wiser than Socrates, and the oracle had replied that there was not. If the deceased Chaerephon's brother was indeed willing to vouch for this story in court (21a), it may have had a basis in fact. But we should not overlook the subtle artifice with which Plato has adapted it to his purpose in what follows. Perplexed by the oracle, Socrates interpreted it to mean that he was 'wiser' than others only in being free from the false conceit of knowledge: if he did not know something, he did not suppose that he did. Once again, Plato makes Socrates an 'example' or model (23b) of an ethical quality, whose importance is constantly reiterated throughout his writings. Deliverance from the false conceit of knowledge is a necessary precondition for learning anything at all. For only those who are made aware of their ignorance will be motivated to remedy it. Socrates, as has been well said, conceived of his divine mission 'as above all the liberation of men's minds from the heavy incubus of an ingrained, self-sustaining ignorance. This liberation held the same priority for him and for Plato as conversion, the sinner's response to divine grace, came to hold for Christians.'[2]

We have already seen how ignorance of that sort had disabled Euthyphro from feeling fear and shame appropriate to his intended action. In the *Defence of Socrates*, likewise, the false conceit of knowledge is a source of misdirected feelings. Those who think they know material wealth, power, prestige, and life itself, to be of greater value than moral excellence will fear the loss of those things more than they fear wrongdoing. In particular, fear of death is diagnosed as thinking one knows something one does not know (29a). The fear is irrational, since it springs from thinking we know death to be an evil, when we do not know that.

Socrates' argument here does not carry conviction. For it is not unreasonable to fear death because we do not know what it holds for us, rather than because we think that we do. But it well illustrates the Socratic belief that our emotional responses need to be conditioned by sound judgements

---

[2] M. J. O'Brien, *The Socratic Paradoxes and the Greek Mind* (Chapel Hill, NC, 1967), 204.

of value: we should fear those things, and only those things, which we have reason to believe are evils. Rationally grounded judgements of value are therefore necessary, and also sufficient, to provide a basis for a proper emotional response. That is why philosophical inquiry matters for the whole conduct of human life. The thought is captured later in Socrates' famous assertion that 'an unexamined life is no life for a human being to live' (38a).

What reason, then, does he have for claiming to *know* that wrongdoing is evil and shameful (29b)? And why, on the strength of that claim, will he persist in examining himself and others, even at risk to his own life? In none of our three works is the claim substantiated. Rather, it functions as a sort of moral axiom, upon which everything else is based, but which itself remains ungrounded. The *Crito* alludes twice (46b–d, 49a–b) to earlier discussions in which it had been established. Its full defence was a major philosophical undertaking, which was to occupy Plato in the *Gorgias* and *Republic*.

In the digression (28b–34b) Socrates argues that, if he were to abandon his quest for moral excellence, he would prove himself guilty of impiety. For he would be disregarding the oracle, fearing death, and thinking himself wise when he was not (29a). Those things would constitute the very offence for which he now stands trial. By implication, he is not guilty of that offence, in that he did heed the oracle, does not fear death, and does not suffer from the false conceit of knowledge. Piety, then, is exemplified in his own actions. We see this again when he insists (35c–d) that the jury should judge his case on its merits: they should not be swayed by emotion to act impiously by violating their oath of office. Thus he can claim to acknowledge the gods in a way that none of his accusers do (35d).

We might therefore imagine that in the *Defence of Socrates* his moral beliefs are founded upon a religious imperative. He compares obedience to God with obedience to military commanders who assigned him to his post on the battlefield (28d–e). Wrongdoing consists in disobedience to his betters, whether human or divine (29b). He practises philosophy as

God's 'servant' (21e, 23b–c). He compares himself with a 'gadfly', attached to the city of Athens by God, to rouse her from her slumbers (30e–31a). He would never abandon that mission, even in return for acquittal (29c–d). These texts would suggest that morally right action, for Socrates, consisted simply in obedience to divine command.

Yet that interpretation would bring the *Defence of Socrates* into conflict with the *Euthyphro*. Socrates could not, consistently with what we have learnt from that dialogue, justify his philosophical activity solely on the ground that it obeyed the will of God. That would be, once again, to make divine command the criterion of morality. But, as the *Euthyphro* shows, that position is untenable for anyone who also wishes to hold that God approves of moral behaviour *because* it is moral, or that God is a moral being himself. Had Socrates been ordered by a dream or oracle to kill one of his young sons, as Abraham in the Old Testament was ordered by God to kill Isaac, it is inconceivable that he would have obeyed. Having faith in God's goodness, he would have refused to accept a religious standard that contravened his ethical one. He would have felt certain that the order, if it genuinely came from God, demanded some alternative interpretation.

But even if the divine will was not the criterion of morality, it was, for Socrates, intimately connected with it. At this point we must take note of a quite extraordinary source of guidance. It is mentioned once in the *Euthyphro* (3b), three times in the *Defence* (31c–d, 40a–c, 41d), and several times elsewhere in Plato. In these texts, Socrates refers to his 'spiritual sign', a mysterious voice that had come to him ever since childhood, warning him not to do things that he was about to do. He expressly calls it 'the sign from God' (40b). Although he says that the sign's warnings often concerned trivial matters, on at least one occasion it must have had a major impact, since it had warned him to stay out of political life (31c–d).

Of special significance here is the inference Socrates draws from the *silence* of the sign on the day of his trial. Although in the past it had frequently warned him when he was about to do anything amiss, at no point had it intervened since he left home that morning, to warn against anything he had said or done (40b, 41d). He takes that as an intimation from God that he had made no mistake, and that the outcome of the trial would prove to be for the best.

The plain implication is that he relied chiefly upon his natural intelligence to guide him in the right direction, and that it normally did so, unless it was countermanded by the sign. Its reliability, throughout his trial, was guaranteed by the fact that the spiritual sign had at no point contradicted it. In the final outcome, it could be trusted to show that even his death would be for the best (40c, 41d). Similarly, in the *Crito*, after arguing at length that he should remain in prison to face death, he can claim that God is guiding him accordingly (54e). The same role for 'intelligence' is attested in the *Phaedo* (98b–99b). Its workings are illustrated from his decision to respect the decision of the Athenian court. In following its dictates, he could be assured that he was doing God's will. His own innate powers of moral reasoning, disciplined by philosophy, and applied with the utmost rigour, could generally be counted upon to place him on the right path.

We might label his position 'religious rationalism'. It places faith in human intelligence as a god-given faculty, in the belief that if used rightly, it will serve as an ethical compass. Euthyphro had said to Socrates airily, 'No doubt you'll handle your case *with intelligence*, as I think I shall handle mine' (3e). Ironically, his prediction regarding Socrates was to prove entirely correct. The dictates of his own 'intelligence' were, to be sure, far more dubious. But then, as we have seen, Plato's purpose in the *Euthyphro* was not to illustrate serious moral deliberation, but to show how the false conceit of knowledge can obstruct it.

The *Crito* affords a complete contrast. For this work is unique among Plato's dialogues in showing Socrates' intelligence being applied to a practical problem of his own. Since it sets a formidable standard of moral argument as well as moral conduct, there is much to be learnt from it.

Like the *Euthyphro*, the *Crito* has a simple structure.

Socrates, awaiting his execution in prison, is visited by his old friend Crito, who brings word that the fatal day is at hand. He urges Socrates to take his last opportunity to escape from gaol. Socrates puts forward his own argument against escaping, and then demolishes the case that Crito has made in favour of it. Most of the Socratic argument is assigned to the personified 'Laws of Athens', who persuade Socrates that it would be wrong for him to escape. Crito finally stops trying to change his friend's mind, and the conversation ends.

Historically, it is quite likely that escape was suggested at some point during Socrates' imprisonment. According to Xenophon (*Memorabilia* iv. 8. 2), his execution was delayed for thirty days after the trial, thus giving plenty of time to plan an escape. Xenophon also testifies that breaking gaol was urged upon Socrates by his friends, and that he refused, asking whether they knew of any place outside Attica that was inaccessible to death (*Defence of Socrates* 23). It is, of course, probable that others besides Crito urged escape. In our dialogue he mentions others who were ready to help (45b), and implies that planning had already taken place (46a). When Socrates reproves Crito for repeatedly urging him to escape (48e), he is probably referring to suggestions made many times in the preceding month.

The *Crito* differs sharply from the *Euthyphro* both in tone and in content. Crito was an old and intimate friend, who had supported Socrates at his trial, offered to guarantee his fine, and tried to secure bail for him. Socrates does not treat him with the studied deference he shows towards Euthyphro. The *Crito* raises no problems of definition, and leaves no loose ends dangling. It is also unlike the *Euthyphro* in reaching a conclusion which could be believed to have guided real action. Even if Euthyphro's lawsuit against his father was a real case, it is hard to believe that Socrates ever dissuaded him from pursuing it. By contrast, it is quite credible that arguments of the sort advanced in the *Crito* should have guided Socrates' decision to remain in gaol.

The *Crito* is also very different from the *Defence*. Crito's personal anguish, contrasted with Socrates' serenity in face of impending death, creates an emotional dynamic quite unlike that of courtroom drama. Although the Laws of Athens indulge in some fervent rhetoric when addressing Socrates, the *Crito* as a whole does not rival the *Defence* in rhetorical power. Socrates no longer has to persuade a large audience. His only object is to convince himself and Crito, through cogent philosophical reasoning, that he is morally bound to accept the sentence of the Athenian court. His obligation to do so is derived from a general obligation of the citizen to obey the law.

Whether the *Crito* is consistent with the *Defence* in demanding obedience to the law has been much debated. To some readers the positions adopted by Socrates in the two works have seemed utterly opposed. In the *Defence* he comes across as a champion of intellectual liberty, an individualist bravely defying the conservative Athenian establishment; whereas in the *Crito* he appears to be advocating the most abject submission of the citizen to state authority. Much scholarly ingenuity has been devoted to explaining away the contradiction. Yet, as we shall see below, the supposed conflict between the two works is illusory.

We may begin with Crito's arguments in favour of escape. He urges, first, that he will be deprived of an irreplaceable companion if Socrates is put to death (44b). Secondly, Socrates' friends will appear in a bad light, since they will be widely thought to have grudged spending money to rescue him (44c). Thirdly, he reassures Socrates on practical matters: he need not be concerned about the expense, and safe haven can easily be found for him in Thessaly (44e–45c). Finally, if Socrates remains in prison, he will be collaborating in his own death, and leaving his three sons as orphans, even though he has a duty to see their upbringing through to the end (45c–d).

Socrates responds, initially, only to the second of these points. Even if most people think poorly of one's friends, one should not be concerned about their opinions. One should care only for the opinions of capable people who will form a correct judgement (44c). His answer to the rest of Crito's case is deferred till later (53a–54b).

The reason for this strategy soon emerges. The points

that Crito has raised about reputation, expenses, and children are characterized as merely 'popular' concerns (48c), by contrast with the arguments that Socrates is about to deploy. According to Socrates (48c–d), the sole question to consider is whether it would be just, or morally right, for him to escape. But if so, why has he troubled to address any of Crito's points at all? Why bother to rebut the suggestion that Socrates' failure to escape will put his friends in a bad light?

The reason is Plato's need to establish the authority of the moral expert. This principle is defended at length with the analogy of the athletic trainer (46e–48a). It provides crucial support for the central argument of the dialogue by underpinning its basic premisses (49a–e). By appealing to expert rather than popular opinion, Plato can also emphasize that a majority deserves no special respect by virtue of its numerical strength. The fact that it can put a man to death is no reason, in logic, for heeding its opinions (44d, 46c, 48a–b, 48d, 49b). Might is not necessarily right.

Socrates first elicits Crito's support for some fundamental moral principles. It is agreed that one should never act unjustly, and therefore never return injustice for injustice (49a–b). Next, treating someone unjustly is equated with ill-treating that person (49c). It follows that one should never ill-treat anyone, even those by whom one has been ill-treated (49d).

This conclusion is then applied to Socrates' relationship with Athens. Crito grants the further principle that one should abide by one's agreements, provided they are just (49e). Socrates suggests that by escaping he will be breaking an agreement he has implicitly made with the city. At this point (50a) the Laws of Athens appear on the scene, and virtually take over the argument for the rest of the dialogue. They are closely associated with the Athenian state, and represent the public interest. In effect, they assume the former role of Socrates, and he assumes that of Crito.

By escaping, the Laws argue, Socrates will be doing his best to destroy them, and consequently the city as a whole (50b). Thus he will be ill-treating the city, and therefore acting unjustly. It will not do for him to answer that the city has treated him unjustly by misjudging his case (50c). For it has already been agreed that ill-treatment of one party by another does not justify the former in retaliating.

The Laws elaborate their position with two closely interwoven lines of argument. First, they develop analogies (50d–51c) between the relation of Socrates to the city and that of offspring to their parents, or of slaves to their masters (50e). In view of the benefits of life and upbringing provided by parents, their offspring owe them obedience. They must submit to parental admonition or punishment, and have no right to answer or strike back (50e–51a). Similarly, the citizen owes obedience to the city in return for the benefits it has provided, and may not strike back.

These analogies do not, at first sight, seem to hold water. The fact that children depend upon their parents for existence, and for many benefits, does not mean that they are morally bound to submit to any punishment their parents see fit to inflict. Nor, obviously, does it license their parents to destroy them altogether. Moreover, once children are grown up, the parents retain no punitive authority at all, although their offspring will still owe them respect and gratitude if they were responsibly brought up. The analogy with the master–slave relationship is equally unconvincing: adult male Athenians were accorded numerous rights denied to slaves. These included the right to emigrate, to which the Laws themselves will call attention (51d). In short, both analogies seem totally inadequate to support their position.

Let us turn, therefore, to their second line of argument. Socrates has, so they claim, made an implicit agreement with them by opting for Athenian citizenship (51d–53a). When he came of age, he had been free to emigrate and live anywhere else he wished. Yet he had not exercised that freedom, but had spent more of his life within the city than almost anyone else (52a–c). His actions, if not his words, have committed him to living according to the city's laws; and that means accepting the sentence imposed upon him, since he has failed to persuade the court either to acquit him or to punish him less severely.

To consider this argument, we must look more closely at the sentence in which the concept of an agreement is first invoked (49e). Socrates suggests, and Crito grants, that one should perform actions one has agreed upon *provided they are just*. What is that proviso designed to rule out? It would clearly rule out agreements to engage in wrongful conduct, for example to kill someone for reward. More to the point, it would rule out agreements into which one party is coerced or tricked or rushed by the other. The Laws will later dismiss such factors as irrelevant in Socrates' case: he has had seventy years in which he was free to leave Athens, if its political and legal system was not to his liking (52e). A further effect of the proviso is to rule out cases where keeping an agreement would, in specific circumstances, result in wrongdoing. For instance, one should break an agreement to return a dangerous weapon to a man who had gone mad since the time when he lent it (*Republic* 331c). In such a case, the original agreement to return the weapon was perfectly just. But one would still have an obligation to break it, in circumstances where keeping it would be clearly wrong.

The obligation to obey the law is therefore not absolute. The *Crito* does not insist upon blind obedience to any and every law, edict, or court-order. It leaves room for a citizen to break his agreement with the state to obey its law *if*, but *only if*, keeping that agreement would result in his doing wrong. The Laws can argue, nevertheless, that that exception does not entitle Socrates to escape from jail. For the sentence of the court does not require him to *act* wrongly himself, but only to *submit to* the wrongdoing of others. Four verbs illustrate this crucial point: 'being beaten', 'being put in bonds', 'being wounded', and 'being killed' (51b). All are in the passive voice. It is not claimed that the citizen has an unconditional obligation to *do* any action the state commands, but only to *suffer* such penalties or hardships as it may see fit to impose.

This point has specific application to sentences imposed by the courts. There was no appeal, under Athenian law, against a decision of the court which convicted Socrates. Nor could the Athenian legal system have granted, any more than ours does, a right to avoid punishment on the ground that an individual had been unjustly convicted. Were there any such right, then, as the Laws say, court judgments would be 'nullified or invalidated by individuals' (50b). There could no more be such a right than there could be a right of the state to punish people found not guilty, on the ground that they had been unjustly acquitted. A legal system must be empowered to dispose of the cases before it with finality. The right to appeal against an unjust conviction does not carry with it a right to avoid punishment when all appeal procedures have been exhausted. All this remains true despite many proven miscarriages of justice. And if the courts cannot always deliver perfect justice in this world, we can only hope for better in the next.

The Laws' analogy with parenthood may now seem more defensible than first appeared. It is not intended to show that a father has the right to treat his dependent offspring as he pleases, or that the offspring have a duty to endure any degree of paternal abuse. Its point is that *just as* a child has no right to strike back at a punishing father, *so* an unjustly treated citizen has no right to strike back at the system that has maltreated him. By escaping, Socrates would be 'striking back'. For by resisting punishment he would be helping to undermine the rule of law itself.

It has been objected to this argument that a single violation of one law by one person goes almost no way towards 'destroying the city'. For there is virtually no chance of its leading to widespread law-breaking, let alone the collapse of civil society. Indeed, a single attempt to break gaol might not even be successful. Yet this objection misses the main thrust of the Laws' argument. For it pays insufficient attention to the specific type of law-breaking against which the argument is primarily directed.

If a given law is widely known to have been broken with impunity, public respect for that law will be diminished. Once discredited, the law will cease to be widely obeyed, and may eventually be abrogated. In Socrates' situation, the law violated by gaol-breaking would be the one requiring that court decisions shall have authority (50b). But no legal system can afford to countenance the discrediting of *that* law, let alone its 'abrogation'. To say, with the Laws of Athens, that 'a great deal could be said on its behalf' is a studied understatement.

For laws not only prohibit or enjoin certain sorts of behaviour; they must also ordain penalties for breaking them. The concepts of law and penalty are inseparable. The 'law' which the Laws of Athens invoke is therefore no ordinary one, but a principle that is basic to any justice system. Let us call it the Enforcement Principle.

If a prominent individual convicted of an offence is known to have escaped punishment, it is predictable that others will try to escape punishment for their offences, taking their cue from the *cause célèbre*. Yet public confidence in a justice system depends upon a belief that breaches of the law will be punished consistently and with certainty. Unless that belief is well founded, threat of punishment will be idle, and will cease to deter. Thus the Enforcement Principle has a unique status. By defying *that* law, Socrates will be striking at *all* laws. That is why the Laws can claim that Socrates will (if he tries to escape) be viewed elsewhere as a would-be subverter of political systems and a destroyer of laws in general (53b–c).

The Laws do not argue, as many have said, by asking what would happen if everybody broke the law. Nor do they claim that any and every violation of any law will tend to destroy that particular law, or cause it to be widely disobeyed. Their central point is, rather, that even a single challenge to the Enforcement Principle will endanger the justice system, by undermining public confidence in its operation. Yet, unless that confidence is sustained, the rule of law must eventually break down. That this is no far-fetched fantasy is evident from the plight of certain modern states, in which the police are too corrupt or the courts too weak to enforce the laws they have on their books.

To defend the Enforcement Principle is by no means to imply that the penal code of any given society must always be meekly accepted by its members, or that they have no moral right to rebel against an oppressive regime. The *Crito* is not preaching craven submission to tyranny, such as that of the Thirty Tyrants or the Third Reich. One may be morally obliged to defy an unjust regime, as Socrates did himself. One may also be morally justified in contesting unduly harsh or cruel methods of law enforcement for specific offences, or protesting at their use in particular cases. But the Enforcement Principle, understood as a general principle underlying all laws, is one that only a consistent anarchist or enemy of the state could reject. For if it is endangered, the whole rule of law is jeopardized. That explains why the Laws of Athens are so adamantly opposed to gaol-breaking, and predict similar reactions from their brother Laws in Hades (54c). It also explains the casuistical distinction they draw between themselves and the human beings by whom Socrates has been wronged (54b–c). For their part, the Laws can claim to have done him no wrong. For he has not been ill-treated by the justice system, but only by the individuals who have abused it to harm him. Yet if he escapes, it will not be those individuals that he harms, but the justice system, and thus the state or commonwealth itself (50a–b).

We saw above that the *Crito* leaves room for disobedience to the law where obedience would require wrongdoing. It could therefore accommodate the sort of law-breaking on conscientious grounds that is nowadays called 'civil disobedience'. Although this was not a feature of Greek political life, the 'moral expert' of the *Crito* could condone and even applaud it, so long as those who engage in it commit no moral wrong, and respect the Enforcement Principle by accepting punishment for their actions. In our own day well-publicized violations of the law by such persons have sometimes rendered it unenforceable. The Canadian abortionist Henry Morgentaler was convicted and gaoled by a Quebec appellate court, following two jury acquittals. After he had served ten months in gaol, juries in his subsequent trials still refused to convict him. Eventually the law restricting abortion was struck down by the Supreme Court of Canada. Clearly, the Enforcement Principle was not jeopardized by Morgentaler's conduct, although the abortion law itself was ultimately destroyed. But if he had attempted to escape from prison, he would have gravely weakened his moral position.

The Laws make exactly that point. They say that, if Socrates escapes to the lawless region of Thessaly, he will make a mockery of the moral stand he had taken at his trial, betraying the very cause for which he had faced conviction

(52c, 53c). It would be as if Morgentaler had broken gaol and fled to a remote region of the Arctic, where no facilities for performing abortions were available. He would then, ironically, have been unable to pursue the very goal for which he had defied the law. For Socrates that irony would have been further compounded. For in his case the prohibited activity was the pursuit of moral excellence through philosophical inquiry. Yet that, of all goals, could not have been pursued at the price of his own integrity. Hence the Laws can ask scathingly what will become, if he escapes, of all his noble arguments advocating moral excellence and law-abiding conduct (52c, 53c, 54a). To attempt escape would be at variance with his moral stand in the *Defence*.

This returns us to the question of consistency between the two works. Can the argument of the *Crito* with respect to obeying the law be squared with Socrates' performance in the courtroom? Surely it can. In the *Defence* itself he repeatedly declares or shows his respect for the law: he has to obey the law, and present his defence (19a); he will obey the law requiring him to be truthful in court (22a); he twice invokes the law in interrogating Meletus (25d, 26a); he has obeyed his legally appointed superiors in battle (28e); he reminds the jurors that they have sworn to try the case according to law (35c). Above all, he describes his own protest, seven years earlier, against an unlawful motion for the collective trial of some naval commanders charged with dereliction of duty (32b–c). His account of that episode is clearly consistent with his position in the *Crito*. For he had spoken out, at great personal risk, in favour of following due legal process.

No less consistent is his refusal to obey an order given him by the Thirty to fetch an innocent man for summary execution (32c–d). Some have urged that the oligarchy was an illegal regime, or that its order was, in any case, an unlawful one, as Xenophon says (*Memorabilia* iv. 4. 3). But Plato's Socrates never makes that point, and the historical question remains moot. Even if the regime and its order were lawful, his defiance remains consistent with his position in the *Crito*. For it was morally wrong to arrest and execute an innocent man (32d). As we have seen, the *Crito* allows for disobedience where compliance would require wrongdoing, provided the disobeyer accepts the consequences. That was exactly Socrates' position. By defying the oligarchy, he says that he knowingly ran a grave risk of death.

But the passage in the *Defence* most often held to conflict with the *Crito* is Socrates' ringing declaration to the jury that, if they were to let him go on condition that he cease his philosophical activities, he would refuse to do so (29c–d, 30b). That has been thought inconsistent with the *Crito*'s teaching that there is an absolute obligation to obey the law. But once again, the *Crito* contains no such teaching. It allows for disobedience on moral grounds, provided the disobeyer is willing to face the consequences. That was Socrates' stance with respect to the practice of philosophy. He would refuse to obey a court-order to give it up, even at the risk of death.

The false impression that the *Crito* teaches an unconditional obligation to obey the law is created, in part, by the imperious eloquence of the Laws of Athens, and the humility with which Socrates receives their lectures. Yet although their arguments finally prevail with him (54d), we need not assume that Plato's 'moral expert' would endorse everything they say. They are right to insist that the Enforcement Principle must be upheld, for the rule of law means nothing without it. Yet Socrates, when speaking in his own person earlier, has repeatedly stressed (46c, 48d, 49b) that threats to property, liberty, and life, which are the instruments of law enforcement, should not prevail at the cost of wrongdoing. Obedience to the law is required only because, and in so far as, the conduct it demands is morally right. Where keeping it would result in wrongdoing, it should be broken, at whatever personal cost. On that point there is no conflict whatever between the *Crito* and the *Defence*.

It is of interest, finally, to compare the *Crito* with the *Euthyphro* on the same issue. In the latter dialogue, we saw, holiness could not be defined in terms of divine approval. The commands of state religion, as interpreted by Euthyphro, could not claim the allegiance of civilized human beings. Moral standards could not be derived from, or overridden by, religious law. A related point holds for the *Crito*. For it derives the state's authority over the citizen from moral principles which are independent of any man-made law (49a–e). Legal obligation in the *Crito*, like religious obligation in the *Euthyphro*, is founded upon a prior conception of what is morally right. Law does not, on such a view, create morality. It only encodes it for agents who are not morally autonomous. Obedience to state law no more makes an action morally right than does obedience to state religion.

If that is correct, the *Euthyphro*, the *Defence of Socrates*, and the *Crito* all alike point towards an objective moral standard that is independent of either divine or human command. That standard is embodied in Socrates himself, for whom the pursuit of moral excellence through philosophical inquiry was tantamount to a religious obligation. The exercise of his intelligence in that pursuit was the faith which he practised. Such is the portrait of his master that Plato has bequeathed in the three works of genius which this volume contains.

NOTE ON THE TEXT
AND TRANSLATION

THE translations in this volume are based upon the revised Oxford Classical Text of Plato, ed. W. S. M. Nicoll *et al.*, vol. i. I am grateful to the editors for allowing me to examine the new text in proof. For the three present works I have noticed thirty-two places where its readings differ from those of J. Burnet's OCT (1900), and more than sixty differences of punctuation. In only a few of these places, however, is the sense affected very substantially. I have followed the new OCT everywhere except at fifteen points indicated in the translation by an obelisk (†). The readings adopted in those places are given in the Textual Notes on page 110.

The page numbers and letters in the margin of the translation derive from the edition of Plato by Stephanus, or Henri Estienne (Geneva, 1578). They are used universally by modern commentators for references to Plato's text, and in the Introduction and notes to this volume. The line numbers in the translation and Textual Notes are those of the revised OCT.

The Explanatory Notes are designed to make the translations intelligible, to explain historical or literary allusions, and to help readers new to these works to follow their arguments. The notes also include select references to passages in Plato where ideas adumbrated in the present works are more fully developed.

The Index of Names includes only historical and mythical figures mentioned by name in Plato's text. Place names are covered in the Explanatory Notes.

The notes and translations owe numerous points to the valuable edition of all three works by J. Burnet (Oxford, 1924), and the magisterial study of the *Defence of Socrates* by E. De Strycker and S. R. Slings (Leiden, 1994).

It is a pleasure to thank Catherine Clarke and Judith Luna of Oxford University Press for their co-operation, and for their kindness to me, while this work was in progress.

I am greatly obliged to D. S. Hutchinson, of Trinity College in the University of Toronto, for generous help. He has read my drafts with meticulous care, and made many suggestions which have improved the work throughout. My former colleague Trudy Govier has commented perceptively on draft translations of the *Euthyphro* and *Crito*, and on a draft of the Introduction. The Introduction has also benefited from discussion of a paper on the *Crito* read to members of the Trent University Philosophy Colloquium. All of these friends have forced me to rethink many questions. Faults and errors that remain are mine alone.

BIBLIOGRAPHICAL NOTE

THE past three decades have witnessed a great resurgence of interest in Socratic philosophy, and therefore a vast proliferation of literature on the *Euthyphro, Defence of Socrates*, and *Crito*. The bibliography has necessarily been limited to a small selection of works in English. They have been chosen to guide readers who are relatively unfamiliar with Plato's writings, or who wish for fuller commentary on the present works than is possible in this volume. More extensive bibliographical guidance will be found in many of the books listed here, particularly in items 30 and 39.

Since it is often worth consulting alternative translations, a selection of these has been listed in items 1–6. They contain English only, except for item 3 which includes a facing-page Greek text. Items 4–6 have useful introductions and explanatory notes.

Items 7 and 8 are, respectively, the former Oxford Classical Text by J. Burnet, and the revised OCT on which the present translations are mainly based.

Item 9 contains a Greek text but no translation. It includes excellent notes, many of which can be read profitably without knowledge of Greek. For the *Defence of Socrates* it should be supplemented by the authoritative literary and philosophical commentary in item 16.

Items 10–24 are stimulating separate studies of each of the three works in this volume.

Items 25 and 26 contain simple outlines of Plato's life and thought; the former includes the famous Seventh Letter upon which all modern reconstructions of his life depend. Item 27 is a short critical assessment of him as a philosopher. Items 28 and 29 provide concise overviews of Socrates and Plato, respectively.

Items 30–9 are of wider scope, but include many chapters and articles devoted to the present works or the issues raised in them. Much useful historical and sociological background for understanding these issues will be found in item 31.

English translations of the most important ancient sources for Socrates other than Plato are given in items 40–3.

SELECT BIBLIOGRAPHY

Complete Works of Plato

1. J. M. Cooper and D. S. Hutchinson, eds., *Plato, Complete Works* (Indianapolis, 1997)
2. E. Hamilton and H. Cairns, eds., *The Collected Dialogues of Plato* (New York, 1961)

Translations of *Euthyphro*, *Defence of Socrates*, and *Crito*

3. H. N. Fowler, in Loeb Classical Library, Plato, vol. i (London and New York, 1914)
4. G. M. A. Grube, in Plato, *Five Dialogues* (Indianapolis, 1981)
5. H. Tredennick and H. Tarrant, in *The Last Days of Socrates* (London, 1993)
6. W. D. Woodhead, in Plato, *Socratic Dialogues* (London, 1953)

Greek Texts

7. J. Burnet, ed., *Platonis Opera*, vol. i (Oxford, 1900)
8. W. S. M. Nicoll *et al.*, eds., *Platonis Opera*, vol. i (Oxford, 1995)

Edition

9. J. Burnet, ed., *Euthyphro, Apology, and Crito* (Oxford, 1924)

Studies of the *Euthyphro*

10. R. E. Allen, *Plato's* Euthyphro *and the Earlier Theory of Forms* (New York, 1970), with a translation
11. J. Beckman, *The Religious Dimension of Socrates' Thought* (Waterloo, Ontario, 1979), esp. ch. 2. 1
12. S. M. Cohen, 'Socrates on the Definition of Piety: *Euthyphro* 10A–11B', *Journal of the History of Philosophy*, 9 (1971), and repr. in item 38, 158–76
13. P. T. Geach, 'Plato's *Euthyphro*: An Analysis and Commentary', *The Monist*, 50 (1966), 369–82
14. C. C. W. Taylor, 'The End of the *Euthyphro*', *Phronesis*, 27 (1982), 109–18

Studies of the *Defence of Socrates*

15. T. C. Brickhouse and N. D. Smith, *Socrates on Trial* (Oxford, 1989)

16. E. De Strycker and S. R. Slings, *Plato's* Apology *of Socrates* (Leiden, New York, Cologne, 1994)
17. C. D. C. Reeve, *Socrates in the* Apology (Indianapolis, 1989)

Studies of the *Crito*

18. R. E. Allen, *Socrates and Legal Obligation* (Minneapolis, 1980), with translations of *Apology* and *Crito*
19. D. Bostock, 'The Interpretation of Plato's *Crito*', *Phronesis*, 35 (1990)
20. R. Kraut, *Socrates and the State* (Princeton, 1984)
21. G. Vlastos, 'Socrates on Political Obedience and Disobedience', *Yale Review*, 42 (1974), 517–34
22. F. C. Wade, 'In Defense of Socrates', *Review of Metaphysics*, 25 (1971), 311–25
23. A. D. Woozley, 'Socrates on Disobeying the Law', in item 38, 299–318
24. —— *Law and Obedience: The Arguments of Plato's Crito* (Chapel Hill, NC, 1979)

Introductions to Socrates and Plato

25. R. S. Bluck, *Plato's Life and Thought, with a Translation of the Seventh Letter* (London, 1949)
26. G. C. Field, *The Philosophy of Plato*, 2nd edn. (Oxford, 1969)
27. R. M. Hare, *Plato*, Past Masters Series (Oxford, 1982)
28. I. G. Kidd, s.v. 'Socrates', *Encyclopaedia of Philosophy*, ed. P. Edwards (New York, 1967), vii. 480–6
29. G. Ryle, s.v. 'Plato', *Encyclopaedia of Philosophy*, ed. P. Edwards (New York, 1967), vi. 320–4

Other Books on Socrates and Plato

30. H. H. Benson, ed., *Essays on the Philosophy of Socrates* (Oxford, 1992)
31. K. J. Dover, *Greek Popular Morality in the Time of Plato and Aristotle* (Oxford, 1974)
32. B. S. Gower and M. C. Stokes, eds., *Socratic Questions* (London and New York, 1992)
33. A. Gómez-Lobo, *The Foundations of Socratic Ethics* (Indianapolis, 1994)
34. W. K. C. Guthrie, *Socrates* (Cambridge, 1971)
35. —— *A History of Greek Philosophy*, vol. iv (Cambridge, 1975)
36. M. J. O'Brien, *The Socratic Paradoxes and the Greek Mind* (Chapel Hill, NC, 1967)

37. A. E. Taylor, *Plato: The Man and his Work* (London, 1929)
38. G. Vlastos, ed., *The Philosophy of Socrates: A Collection of Critical Essays* (New York, 1971)
39. —— *Socrates: Ironist and Moral Philosopher* (Cambridge, 1991)

Ancient Sources on Socrates

40. E. C. Marchant and O. J. Todd, trans., Xenophon, *Memorabilia, Oeconomicus, Symposium*, and *Apology*, Loeb Classical Library (Cambridge, Mass., and London, 1923)
41. H. Tredennick and R. Waterfield, eds., *Xenophon: Conversations of Socrates* (Harmondsworth, 1990)
42. J. Henderson, trans., Aristophanes, *Clouds* (Newburyport, Mass., 1992)
43. R. D. Hicks, trans., Diogenes Laertius, *Lives of the Philosophers*, Loeb Classical Library (Cambridge, Mass., and London, 1959), 2 vols.

EUTHYPHRO

EUTHYPHRO

EUTHYPHRO. What trouble has arisen, Socrates, to make   2a
  you leave your haunts in the Lyceum,* and spend your
  time here today at the Porch of the King Archon?*
  Surely you of all people don't have some sort of lawsuit
  before him, as I do?
SOCRATES. Well no; Athenians, at any rate, don't call it a   5
  lawsuit, Euthyphro—they call it an indictment.*
EUTHYPHRO. What's that you say? Somebody must have   b
  indicted you, since I can't imagine your doing that to
  anyone else.
SOCRATES. No, I haven't.
EUTHYPHRO. But someone else has indicted you?
SOCRATES. Exactly.   5
EUTHYPHRO. Who is he?
SOCRATES. I hardly even know the man myself, Euthyphro;
  I gather he's young and unknown—but I believe he's
  named Meletus. He belongs to the Pitthean deme*—
  can you picture a Meletus from that deme, with straight   10
  hair, not much of a beard, and a rather aquiline nose?
EUTHYPHRO. No, I can't picture him, Socrates. But tell   c
  me, what is this indictment he's brought against you?
SOCRATES. The indictment? I think it does him credit. To
  have made such a major discovery is no mean achievement for one so young: he claims to know how the
  young people are being corrupted, and who are corrupt-   5
  ing them. He's probably a smart fellow; and noticing
  that in my ignorance I'm corrupting his contempor-
  aries, he is going to denounce me to the city, as if to
  his mother.

  Actually, he seems to me to be the only one who's   d
  making the right start in politics: it *is* right to make it
  one's first concern that the young should be as good as
  possible, just as a good farmer is likely to care first for
  the young plants, and only later for the others. And so
  Meletus is no doubt first weeding out those of us who   3a

3

are 'ruining the shoots of youth', as he puts it. Next
after this, he'll take care of the older people, and will
obviously bring many great blessings to the city: at least

5   that would be the natural outcome after such a start.

EUTHYPHRO. So I could wish, Socrates, but I'm afraid the
opposite may happen: in trying to injure you, I really
think he's making a good start at damaging the city.*
Tell me, what does he claim you are actually doing to
corrupt the young?

b   SOCRATES. Absurd things, by the sound of them, my admirable friend: he says that I'm an inventor of gods; and
for inventing strange gods, while failing to recognize the
gods of old, he's indicted me on their behalf, so he says.

5   EUTHYPHRO. I see, Socrates; it's because you say that your
spiritual sign* visits you now and then. So he's brought
this indictment against you as a religious innovator, and
he's going to court to misrepresent you, knowing that
such things are easily misrepresented before the pub-

c   lic. Why, it's just the same with me: whenever I speak
in the Assembly* on religious matters and predict the
future for them, they laugh at me as if I were crazy;
and yet not one of my predictions has failed to come
true. Even so, they always envy people like ourselves. We

5   mustn't worry about them, though—we must face up to
them.

SOCRATES. Yes, my dear Euthyphro, being laughed at is
probably not important. You know, Athenians don't
much care, it seems to me, if they think someone clever,
so long as he's not imparting his wisdom to others; but
once they think he's making other people clever, then

d   they get angry—whether from envy, as you say, or for
some other reason.

EUTHYPHRO. In that case I don't much want to test their
feelings towards me.

5   SOCRATES. Well, they probably think you give sparingly
of yourself, and aren't willing to impart your wisdom.
But in my case, I fear my benevolence* makes them
think I give all that I have, by speaking without reserve
to every comer; not only do I speak without charge, but

I'd gladly be out of pocket if anyone cares to listen to me. So, as I was just saying, if they were only going to laugh at me, as you say they laugh at you, it wouldn't be bad sport if they passed the time joking and laughing in the courtroom. But if they're going to be serious, then there's no knowing how things will turn out—except for you prophets.

EUTHYPHRO. Well, I dare say it will come to nothing, Socrates. No doubt you'll handle your case with intelligence,* as I think I shall handle mine.

SOCRATES. And what is this case of yours, Euthyphro? Are you defending or prosecuting?

EUTHYPHRO. Prosecuting.

SOCRATES. Whom?

EUTHYPHRO. Once again, someone whom I'm thought crazy to be prosecuting.

SOCRATES. How's that? Are you chasing a bird on the wing?*

EUTHYPHRO. The bird is long past flying: in fact, he's now quite elderly.

SOCRATES. And who is he?

EUTHYPHRO. My father.

SOCRATES. *What?* Your own *father!*

EUTHYPHRO. Precisely.

SOCRATES. But what is the charge? What is the case about?

EUTHYPHRO. It's a case of murder, Socrates.

SOCRATES. Good heavens above! Well, Euthyphro, most people are obviously ignorant of where the right lies in such a case, since I can't imagine any ordinary person taking that action.† It must need someone pretty far advanced in wisdom.

EUTHYPHRO. Goodness yes, Socrates. Far advanced indeed!

SOCRATES. And is your father's victim one of your relatives? Obviously, he must be—you'd hardly be prosecuting him for murder on behalf of a stranger.

EUTHYPHRO. It's ridiculous, Socrates, that you should think it makes any difference whether the victim was a stranger or a relative, and not see that the sole consideration is whether or not the slaying was lawful. If it was, one

10
c

should leave the slayer alone; but if it wasn't, one should prosecute, even if the slayer shares one's own hearth and board—because the pollution is just the same, if you knowingly associate with such a person, and fail to cleanse yourself and him by taking legal action.

In point of fact, the victim was a day-labourer of mine: when we were farming in Naxos,* he was working there on our estate. He had got drunk, flown into a rage with one of our servants, and butchered him. So my father had him bound hand and foot, and flung into a ditch; he then sent a messenger here to find out from the religious authority* what should be done. In the mean time, he disregarded his captive, and neglected him as a murderer, thinking it wouldn't much matter even if he died. And that was just what happened: the man died of hunger and cold, and from his bonds, before the messenger got back from the authority.

That's why my father and other relatives are now upset with me, because I'm prosecuting him for murder on a murderer's behalf. According to them, he didn't even kill him. And even if he was definitely a killer, they say that, since the victim was a murderer, I shouldn't be troubled on such a fellow's behalf—because it is unholy for a son to prosecute his father for murder. Little do they know, Socrates, of religious law about what is holy and unholy.

SOCRATES. But heavens above, Euthyphro, do you think *you* have such exact knowledge of religion, of things holy and unholy? Is it so exact that in the circumstances you describe, you aren't afraid that, by bringing your father to trial, you might prove guilty of unholy conduct yourself?

EUTHYPHRO. Yes it is, Socrates; in fact I'd be good for nothing, and Euthyphro wouldn't differ at all from the common run of men, unless I had exact knowledge of all such matters.

SOCRATES. Why then, my admirable Euthyphro, my best course is to become your student, and to challenge Meletus on this very point before his indictment is heard.

6

I could say that even in the past I always used to set a
high value upon religious knowledge; and that now,
because he says I've gone astray by free-thinking and
religious innovation, I have become your student.

'Meletus,' I could say: 'if you agree that Euthyphro is   b
an expert on such matters, then you should regard me
as orthodox too, and drop the case. But if you don't
admit that, then proceed against that teacher of mine,
not me, for corrupting the elderly—namely, myself and
his own father—myself by his teaching, and his father   5
by admonition and punishment.'

Then, if he didn't comply and drop the charge, or
indict you in my place, couldn't I repeat in court the
very points on which I'd already challenged him?

EUTHYPHRO. By God, Socrates, if he tried indicting me, I
fancy I'd soon find his weak spots; and we'd have *him*   c
being discussed in the courtroom long before I was.

SOCRATES. Why yes, dear friend, I realize that, and that's
why I'm eager to become your student. I know that this   5
Meletus, amongst others no doubt, doesn't even seem
to notice you; it's me he's detected so keenly and so
readily that he can charge me with impiety.

So now, for goodness' sake, tell me what you were
just maintaining you knew for sure. What sort of thing
would you say that the pious and the impious are,
whether in murder or in other matters? Isn't the holy   d
itself the same as itself in every action? And conversely,
isn't the unholy* the exact opposite of the holy, in itself
similar to itself,* or possessed of a single character,* in
anything at all that is going to be unholy?†   5

EUTHYPHRO. Indeed it is, Socrates.

SOCRATES. Tell me, then, what do you say that the holy
is? And the unholy?

EUTHYPHRO. All right, I'd say that the holy is just what
I'm doing now: prosecuting wrongdoers, whether in
cases of murder or temple-robbery, or those guilty of   10
any other such offence, be they one's father or mother   e
or anyone else whatever; and failing to prosecute is
unholy.

See how strong my evidence is, Socrates, that this is
the law—evidence I've already given others that my conduct was correct: one must not tolerate an impious man,
no matter who he may happen to be. The very people
who recognize Zeus as best and most righteous of the
gods admit that he put his father in bonds* for wrong-
fully gobbling up his children; and that that father in
turn castrated *his* father for similar misdeeds. And yet
they are angry with me, because I'm prosecuting *my*
father as a wrongdoer. Thus, they contradict themselves
in what they say about the gods and about me.

SOCRATES. Could this be the reason why I'm facing indictment, Euthyphro? Is it because when people tell such
stories of the gods, I somehow find them hard to accept?
That, I suppose, is why some will say that I've gone
astray. But now, if these stories convince you—with
your great knowledge of such matters—then it seems
that the rest of us must accept them as well. What can
we possibly say, when by our own admission we know
nothing of these matters? But tell me, in the name of
friendship, do you really believe that those things happened as described?

EUTHYPHRO. Yes, and even more remarkable things, Socrates, of which most people are ignorant.

SOCRATES. And do you believe that the gods actually make
war upon one another?* That they have terrible feuds
and fights, and much more of the sort related by our
poets, and depicted by our able painters, to adorn our
temples—especially the robe which is covered with such
adornments, and gets carried up to the Acropolis at the
great Panathenaean festival?* Are we to say that those
stories are true, Euthyphro?

EUTHYPHRO. Not only those, Socrates, but as I was just
saying, I'll explain to you many further points about
religion, if you'd like, which I'm sure you'll be astonished to hear.

SOCRATES. I shouldn't be surprised. But explain them to
me at leisure some other time. For now, please try to
tell me more clearly what I was just asking. You see, my

friend, you didn't instruct me properly when I asked my
earlier question: I asked what the holy might be, but
you told me that the holy was what you are now doing,
prosecuting your father for murder.

EUTHYPHRO. Yes, and there I was right, Socrates.   5

SOCRATES. Maybe. Yet surely, Euthyphro, there are many
other things you call holy as well.

EUTHYPHRO. So there are.

SOCRATES. And do you recall that I wasn't urging you to
teach me about one or two of those many things that   10
are holy, but rather about the form itself* whereby all
holy things are holy? Because you said, I think, that it
was by virtue of a single character that unholy things are   e
unholy, and holy things are holy. Don't you remember?

EUTHYPHRO. Yes, I do.

SOCRATES. Then teach me about that character, about what
it might be, so that by fixing my eye upon it and using   5
it as a model, I may call holy any action of yours or
another's, which conforms to it, and may deny to be
holy whatever does not.

EUTHYPHRO. All right, if that's what you want, Socrates,
that's what I'll tell you.

SOCRATES. Yes, that *is* what I want.   10

EUTHYPHRO. In that case, what is agreeable to the gods is
holy, and what is not agreeable to them is unholy.   7a

SOCRATES. Splendid, Euthyphro!—You've given just the
sort of answer I was looking for. Mind you, I don't yet
know whether it's correct, but obviously you will go on
to show that what you say is true.   5

EUTHYPHRO. I certainly will.

SOCRATES. All right then, let's consider what it is we're
saying. A thing or a person loved-by-the-gods is holy,
whereas something or someone hated-by-the-gods* is
unholy; and the holy isn't the same as the unholy, but
is the direct opposite of it. Isn't that what we're saying?   10

EUTHYPHRO. Exactly.

SOCRATES. And does it seem well put?

EUTHYPHRO. I think so, Socrates.   b

SOCRATES. And again, Euthyphro, the gods quarrel and

have their differences, and there is mutual hostility amongst them. Hasn't that been said as well?

5 EUTHYPHRO. Yes, it has.

SOCRATES. Well, on what matters do their differences produce hostility and anger, my good friend? Let's look at it this way. If we differed, you and I, about which of two things was more numerous, would our difference on these questions make us angry and hostile towards
10 one another? Or would we resort to counting in such
c disputes, and soon be rid of them?*

EUTHYPHRO. We certainly would.

SOCRATES. Again, if we differed about which was larger and smaller, we'd soon put an end to our difference by
5 resorting to measurement, wouldn't we?

EUTHYPHRO. That's right.

SOCRATES. And we would decide a dispute about which was heavier and lighter, presumably, by resorting to weighing.

EUTHYPHRO. Of course.

10 SOCRATES. Then what sorts of questions would make us angry and hostile towards one another, if we differed about them and were unable to reach a decision? Perhaps you can't say offhand. But consider my suggestion,
d that they are questions of what is just and unjust,* honourable and dishonourable, good and bad. Aren't those the matters on which our disagreement and our inability to reach a satisfactory decision occasionally make
5 enemies of us, of you and me, and of people in general?

EUTHYPHRO. Those are the differences, Socrates, and that's what they're about.

SOCRATES. And what about the gods, Euthyphro? If they really do differ, mustn't they differ about those same
10 things?

EUTHYPHRO. They certainly must.

e SOCRATES. Then, by your account, noble Euthyphro, different gods also regard different things as just, or as honourable and dishonourable, good and bad; because unless they differed on those matters, they wouldn't quarrel, would they?

EUTHYPHRO. Correct.   5

SOCRATES. And again, the things each of them regards as
honourable, good, or just, are also the things they love,
while it's the opposites of those things that they hate.

EUTHYPHRO. Indeed.

SOCRATES. And yet it's the same things, according to you,   10
that some gods consider just, and others unjust, about   8a
which their disputes lead them to quarrel and make war
upon one another. Isn't that right?

EUTHYPHRO. It is.

SOCRATES. Then the same things, it appears, are both hated
and loved by the gods, and thus the same things would
be both hated-by-the-gods and loved-by-the-gods.   5

EUTHYPHRO. It does appear so.

SOCRATES. So by this argument, Euthyphro, the same things
would be both holy and unholy.

EUTHYPHRO. It looks that way.

SOCRATES. So then you haven't answered my question, my   10
admirable friend. You see, I wasn't asking what selfsame thing* proves to be at once holy and unholy. And
yet something which is loved-by-the-gods is apparently
also hated-by-the-gods. Hence, as regards your present   b
action in punishing your father, Euthyphro, it wouldn't
be at all surprising if you were thereby doing something
agreeable to Zeus but odious to Cronus and Uranus,*
or pleasing to Hephaestus but odious to Hera; and likewise for any other gods who may differ from one another   5
on the matter.

EUTHYPHRO. Yes Socrates, but I don't think any of the
gods do differ from one another on this point, at least:
whoever has unjustly killed another should be punished.

SOCRATES. Really? Well, what about human beings,   10
Euthyphro? Have you never heard any of them arguing   c
that someone who has killed unjustly, or acted unjustly
in some other way, should not be punished?

EUTHYPHRO. Why yes, they are constantly arguing that
way, in the lawcourts as well as elsewhere: people who
act unjustly in all sorts of ways will do or say anything   5
to escape punishment.

SOCRATES. But do they admit acting unjustly, Euthyphro, yet still say, despite that admission, that they shouldn't be punished?

EUTHYPHRO. No, they don't say that at all.

10 SOCRATES. So it isn't just anything that they will say or do. This much, I imagine, they don't dare to say or

d argue: if they act unjustly, they should not be punished. Rather, I imagine, they deny acting unjustly, don't they?

EUTHYPHRO. True.

SOCRATES. Then they don't argue that one who acts un-

5 justly should not be punished; but they do argue, maybe, about who it was that acted unjustly, and what he did, and when.

EUTHYPHRO. True.

SOCRATES. Then doesn't the very same thing also apply to the gods—if they really do quarrel about just and unjust actions, as your account suggests, and if each

10 party says that the other acts unjustly, while the other denies it? Because surely, my admirable friend, no one

e among gods or men dares to claim that anyone should go unpunished who *has* acted unjustly.*

EUTHYPHRO. Yes, what you say is true, Socrates, at least on the whole.

5 SOCRATES. Rather, Euthyphro, I think it is the individual act that causes arguments among gods as well as human beings—if gods really do argue: it is with regard to some particular action that they differ, some saying it was done justly, while others say it was unjust. Isn't that so?

10 EUTHYPHRO. Indeed.

9a SOCRATES. Then please, my dear Euthyphro, instruct me too, that I may grow wiser. When a hired man has committed murder, has been put in bonds by the master of

5 his victim, and has died from those bonds before his captor can find out from the authorities what to do about him, what proof have you that all gods regard that man as having met an unjust death? Or that it is right for a son to prosecute his father and press a charge

b of murder on behalf of such a man? Please try to show me plainly that all gods undoubtedly regard that action

in those circumstances as right. If you can show that
to my satisfaction, I'll never stop singing the praises of
your wisdom.

EUTHYPHRO. Well, that may be no small task, Socrates,   5
though I *could* of course prove it to you quite plainly.

SOCRATES. I see. You must think me a slower learner than
the jury, because obviously you will show them that the
acts in question were unjust, and that all the gods hate
such things.

EUTHYPHRO. I will show that very clearly, Socrates, pro-   10
vided they listen while I'm talking.

SOCRATES. They'll listen all right, so long as they approve   c
of what you're saying.

But while you were talking, I reflected and put to
myself this question: 'Even suppose Euthyphro were
to instruct me beyond any doubt that the gods all do
regard such a death as unjust, what more have I learnt   5
from him about what the holy and the unholy might
be? This particular deed would be hated-by-the-gods,
apparently; yet it became evident just now that the holy
and unholy were not defined in that way, since what is
hated-by-the-gods proved to be loved-by-the-gods as
well.'

So I'll let you off on that point, Euthyphro; let *all* the
gods consider it unjust, if you like, and let *all* of them   d
hate it. Is this the correction we are now making in
our account: whatever *all* the gods hate is unholy, and
whatever they *all* love is holy; and whatever some gods
love but others hate is neither or both? Is that how you
would now have us define the holy and the unholy?   5

EUTHYPHRO. What objection could there be, Socrates?

SOCRATES. None on my part, Euthyphro. But consider your
own view, and see whether, by making that suggestion,
you will most easily teach me what you promised.   10

EUTHYPHRO. Very well, I would say that the holy is what-   e
ever all the gods love; and its opposite, whatever all the
gods hate, is unholy.

SOCRATES. Then shall we examine that in turn, Euthyphro,
and see whether it is well put? Or shall we let it pass, and   5

accept it from ourselves and others? Are we to agree with a position merely on the strength of someone's say-so, or should we examine what the speaker is saying?

EUTHYPHRO. We should examine it. Even so, for my part I believe that this time our account is well put.

10a SOCRATES. We shall soon be better able to tell, sir. Just consider the following question: is the holy loved by the gods because it is holy? Or is it holy because it is loved?*

EUTHYPHRO. I don't know what you mean, Socrates.

5 SOCRATES. All right, I'll try to put it more clearly. We speak of a thing's 'being carried' or 'carrying', of its 'being led' or 'leading', of its 'being seen' or 'seeing'. And you understand, don't you, that all such things are different from each other, and how they differ?*

EUTHYPHRO. Yes, I think I understand.

10 SOCRATES. And again, isn't there something that is 'being loved', while that which loves is different from it?

EUTHYPHRO. Of course.

b SOCRATES. Then tell me whether something in a state of 'being carried' is in that state because someone is carrying it,* or for some other reason.

EUTHYPHRO. No, that is the reason.

SOCRATES. And something in a state of 'being led' is so because someone is leading it, and something in a state 5 of 'being seen' is so because someone is seeing it?

EUTHYPHRO. Certainly.

SOCRATES. Then someone does not see a thing because it is in a state of 'being seen', but on the contrary, it is in that state because someone is seeing it; nor does someone lead a thing because it is in a state of 'being led', 10 but rather it is in that state because someone is leading it; nor does someone carry a thing because it is in a state of 'being carried', but it is in that state because c someone is carrying it. Is my meaning quite clear, Euthyphro? What I mean is this:* if something gets into a certain state or is affected in a certain way, it does not get into that state because it possesses it; rather, it possesses that state because it gets into it; nor is it thus affected because it is in that condition; rather, it is in

that condition because it is thus affected. Don't you
agree with that?   5

EUTHYPHRO. Yes, I do.

SOCRATES. Again, 'being loved' is a case of either being in
a certain state or being in a certain condition because of
some agent?*

EUTHYPHRO. Certainly.

SOCRATES. Then this case is similar to our previous ex-   10
amples: it is not because it is in a state of 'being loved'
that an object is loved by those who love it; rather, it is
in that state because it is loved by them. Isn't that right?

EUTHYPHRO. It must be.

SOCRATES. Now what are we saying about the holy,   d
Euthyphro? On your account, doesn't it consist in being
loved by all the gods?

EUTHYPHRO. Yes.

SOCRATES. Is that because it is holy, or for some other
reason?

EUTHYPHRO. No, that is the reason.*   5

SOCRATES. So it is loved because it is holy, not holy because it is loved.

EUTHYPHRO. So it seems.

SOCRATES. By contrast, what is loved-by-the-gods* is in
that state—namely, being loved-by-the-gods—because
the gods love it.†   10

EUTHYPHRO. Of course.

SOCRATES. Then what is loved-by-the-gods is not the holy,
Euthyphro, nor is the holy what is loved-by-the-gods, as
you say, but they differ from each other.

EUTHYPHRO. How so, Socrates?   e

SOCRATES. Because we are agreed, aren't we, that the holy
is loved because it is holy, not holy because it is loved?

EUTHYPHRO. Yes.   5

SOCRATES. Whereas what is loved-by-the-gods is so because the gods love it. It is loved-by-the-gods by virtue
of their loving it; it is not because it is in that state that
they love it.

EUTHYPHRO. That's true.

SOCRATES. But if what is loved-by-the-gods and the holy   10

11a were the same thing,* Euthyphro, then if the holy were loved because it is holy, what is loved-by-the-gods would be loved because it is loved-by-the-gods; and again, if what is loved-by-the-gods were loved-by-the-gods because they love it, then the holy would be holy because they love it. In actual fact, however, you can see that the two of them are related in just the opposite way, as two entirely different things: one of them is lovable

5 because they love it, whereas the other they love for the reason that it is lovable.*

And so, Euthyphro, when you are asked what the holy might be, it looks as if you'd prefer not to explain its essence to me, but would rather tell me one of its properties*—namely, that the holy has the property of

b being loved by all the gods; but you still haven't told me what it *is*.

So please don't hide it from me, but start again and tell me what the holy might be—whether it is loved by the gods or possesses any other property, since we won't disagree about that.* Out with it now, and tell me what

5 the holy and the unholy are.

EUTHYPHRO. The trouble is, Socrates, that I can't tell you what I have in mind, because whatever we suggest keeps moving around somehow, and refuses to stay put where we established it.

SOCRATES. My ancestor Daedalus* seems to be the author

c of your words, Euthyphro. Indeed, if they were my own words and suggestions, you might make fun of me, and say that it's because of my kinship with him that my works of art in conversation run away* from me too, and won't stay where they're placed. But in fact those

5 suggestions are your own; and so you need a different joke, because you're the one for whom they won't stay put—as you realize yourself.

EUTHYPHRO. No, I think it's much the same joke that is called for by what we said, Socrates: I'm not the one

10 who makes them move around and not stay put. I think

d you're the Daedalus because, as far as I'm concerned, they would have kept still.

16

SOCRATES. It looks then, my friend, as if I've grown this
much more accomplished at my craft than Daedalus
himself: he made only his own works move around,   5
whereas I do it, apparently, to those of others besides
my own. And indeed the really remarkable feature of
my craft is that I'm an expert at it without even want-
ing to be. You see, I'd prefer to have words stay put for
me, immovably established, than to acquire the wealth   e
of Tantalus and the skill of Daedalus combined.

But enough of this. Since I think you are being feeble,*
I'll join you myself in an effort to help you instruct me
about the holy. Don't give up too soon, now. Just consider whether you think that everything that is holy must   5
be just.

EUTHYPHRO. Yes, I do.

SOCRATES. Well then, is everything that is just holy? Or is
everything that is holy just, but not everything that is   12a
just holy? Is part of it holy, and part of it something
else?*

EUTHYPHRO. I can't follow what you're saying, Socrates.

SOCRATES. And yet you are as much my superior in youth
as you are in wisdom. But as I say, your wealth of wis-   5
dom has enfeebled you. So pull yourself together, my
dear sir—it really isn't hard to see what I mean: it's just
the opposite of what the poet meant who composed these
verses:

With Zeus, who wrought it and who generated all these
    things,
You cannot quarrel;† for where there is fear, there is also b
    shame.*

I disagree with that poet. Shall I tell you where?

EUTHYPHRO. By all means.

SOCRATES. I don't think that 'where there is fear, there
is also shame'; because many people, I take it, dread
illnesses, poverty, and many other such things. Yet al-   5
though they dread them, they are not ashamed of what
they fear. Don't you agree?

EUTHYPHRO. Certainly.

SOCRATES. On the other hand, where there is shame, there
is also fear: doesn't anyone who is ashamed and embarrassed by a certain action both fear and dread a reputation for wickedness?*

EUTHYPHRO. Indeed he does.

SOCRATES. Then it isn't right to say that 'where there is
fear, there is also shame'; nevertheless, where there is
shame there is also fear, even though shame is not found
everywhere there is fear. Fear is broader than shame, I
think, since shame is one kind of fear, just as odd is one
kind of number. Thus, it is not true that wherever there
is number there is also odd, although it is true that
where there is odd, there is also number. You follow me
now, presumably?

EUTHYPHRO. Perfectly.

SOCRATES. Well, that's the sort of thing I meant just now:
I was asking, 'Is it true that wherever a thing is just, it
is also holy? Or is a thing just wherever it is holy, but
not holy wherever it is just?' In other words, isn't the
holy part of what is just? Is that what we're to say, or
do you disagree?

EUTHYPHRO. No, let's say that: your point strikes me as
correct.

SOCRATES. Then consider the next point: if the holy is one
part of what is just, it would seem that we need to find
out which part it might be. Now, if you asked me about
one of the things just mentioned, for example, which
kind of number is even, and what sort of number it
might be, I'd say that it's any number which is not
scalene but isosceles.* Would you agree?

EUTHYPHRO. I would.

SOCRATES. Now you try to instruct me, likewise, which
part of what is just is holy. Then we'll be able to tell
Meletus not to treat us unjustly any longer, or indict us
for impiety, because I've now had proper tuition from
you about what things are pious or holy, and what are
not.

EUTHYPHRO. Well then, in my view, the part of what is
just that is pious or holy has to do with ministering to

the gods, while the rest of it has to do with ministering to human beings.

SOCRATES. Yes, I think you put that very well, Euthyphro. I am still missing one small detail, however. You see, I 13a don't yet understand this 'ministering' of which you speak. You surely don't mean 'ministering' to the gods in the same sense as 'ministering' to other things. That's how we talk, isn't it? We say, for example, that not everyone understands how to minister to horses, but only the horse-trainer. Isn't that right? 5

EUTHYPHRO. Certainly.

SOCRATES. Because, surely, horse-training is ministering to horses.

EUTHYPHRO. Yes.

SOCRATES. Nor, again, does everyone know how to minister to dogs, but only the dog-trainer. 10

EUTHYPHRO. Just so.

SOCRATES. Because, of course, dog-training is ministering to dogs.

EUTHYPHRO. Yes. b

SOCRATES. And again, cattle-farming is ministering to cattle.

EUTHYPHRO. Certainly.

SOCRATES. And holiness or piety is ministering to the gods, Euthyphro? Is that what you're saying? 5

EUTHYPHRO. It is.

SOCRATES. Well, doesn't all ministering achieve the same thing? I mean something like this: it aims at some good or benefit for its object. Thus, you may see that horses, when they are being ministered to by horse-training, are benefited and improved. Or don't you think they are? 10

EUTHYPHRO. Yes, I do.

SOCRATES. And dogs, of course, are benefited by dog-training, and cattle by cattle-farming, and the rest like- c wise. Or do you suppose that ministering is for harming its objects?

EUTHYPHRO. Goodness, no!

SOCRATES. So it's for their benefit?

EUTHYPHRO. Of course. 5

SOCRATES. Then, if holiness is ministering to the gods, does it benefit the gods and make them better? And would you grant that whenever you do something holy, you're making some god better?

10 EUTHYPHRO. Heavens, no!

SOCRATES. No, I didn't think you meant that, Euthyphro—

d far from it—but that was the reason why I asked what sort of ministering to the gods you did mean. I didn't think you meant that sort.

EUTHYPHRO. Quite right, Socrates: that's not the sort of thing I mean.

5 SOCRATES. Very well, but then what sort of ministering to the gods would holiness be?

EUTHYPHRO. The sort which slaves give to their masters, Socrates.

SOCRATES. I see. Then it would appear to be some sort of service to the gods.

EUTHYPHRO. Exactly.

10 SOCRATES. Now could you tell me what result is achieved by service to doctors? It would be health, wouldn't it?

EUTHYPHRO. It would.

e SOCRATES. And what about service to shipwrights? What result is achieved in their service?

EUTHYPHRO. Obviously, Socrates, the construction of ships.

SOCRATES. And service to builders, of course, achieves the construction of houses.

5 EUTHYPHRO. Yes.

SOCRATES. Then tell me, good fellow, what product would be achieved by service to the gods? You obviously know, since you claim religious knowledge superior to any man's.

10 EUTHYPHRO. Yes, and there I'm right, Socrates.

SOCRATES. Then tell me, for goodness' sake, just what that splendid task is which the gods accomplish by using our services?

EUTHYPHRO. They achieve many fine things, Socrates.

14a SOCRATES. Yes, and so do generals, my friend. Yet you could easily sum up their achievement as the winning of victory in war, couldn't you?

EUTHYPHRO. Of course.

SOCRATES. And farmers too. They achieve many fine things,   5
I believe. Yet they can be summed up as the production
of food from the earth.

EUTHYPHRO. Certainly.

SOCRATES. And now how about the many fine achievements of the gods? How can their work be summed up?   10

EUTHYPHRO. I've already told you a little while ago, Socrates, that it's a pretty big job to learn the exact truth   b
on all these matters. But I will simply tell you this much:
if one has expert knowledge of the words and deeds
that gratify the gods through prayer and sacrifice, those
are the ones that are holy: such practices are the salva-
tion of individual families, along with the common good   5
of cities; whereas practices that are the opposite of gratifying are impious ones, which of course upset and ruin
everything.

SOCRATES. I'm sure you could have given a summary answer
to my question far more briefly, Euthyphro, if you'd
wanted to. But you're not eager to teach me—that's clear   c
because you've turned aside just when you were on the
very brink of the answer.* If you'd given it, I would
have learnt properly from you about holiness by now.
But as it is, the questioner must follow wherever the
person questioned may lead him.* So, once again, what   5
are you saying that the holy or holiness is? Didn't you
say it was some sort of expertise in sacrifice and prayer?

EUTHYPHRO. Yes, I did.

SOCRATES. And sacrifice is giving things to the gods, while
prayer is asking things of them?

EUTHYPHRO. Exactly, Socrates.   10

SOCRATES. So, by that account, holiness will be expertise   d
in asking from the gods and giving to them.

EUTHYPHRO. You've gathered my meaning beautifully,
Socrates.

SOCRATES. Yes, my friend, that's because I'm greedy for
your wisdom, and apply my intelligence to it, so that
what you say won't fall wasted to the ground. But tell   5
me, what is this service to the gods? You say it is asking
from them, and giving to them?

EUTHYPHRO. I do.

SOCRATES. Well, would asking rightly be asking for things
10   we need from them?

EUTHYPHRO. Why, what else could it be?

e   SOCRATES. And conversely, giving rightly would be giving
them in return things that they do, in fact, need from
us. Surely it would be inept to give anybody things he
didn't need, wouldn't it?

5   EUTHYPHRO. True, Socrates.

SOCRATES. So then holiness would be a sort of skill in
mutual trading between gods and mankind?

EUTHYPHRO. Trading, yes, if that's what you prefer to
call it.*

SOCRATES. I don't prefer anything unless it is actually true.
10   But tell me, what benefit do the gods derive from the
gifts they receive from us? What they give, of course,
15a   is obvious to anyone—since we possess nothing good
which they don't give us. But how are they benefited by
what they receive from us? Do we get so much the
better bargain in our trade with them that we receive
all the good things from them, while they receive none
5   from us?

EUTHYPHRO. Come, Socrates, do you really suppose that
the gods are benefited by what they receive from us?

SOCRATES. Well if not, Euthyphro, what ever would they
be, these gifts of ours to the gods?

10   EUTHYPHRO. What else do you suppose but honour and
reverence, and—as I said just now—what is gratifying
to them?

b   SOCRATES. So the holy is gratifying, but not beneficial or
loved by the gods?*

EUTHYPHRO. I imagine it is the most loved of all things.

SOCRATES. Then, once again, it seems that this is what the
5   holy is: what is loved by the gods.*

EUTHYPHRO. Absolutely.

SOCRATES. Well now, if you say that, can you wonder if
you find that words won't keep still for you, but walk
about? And will you blame me as the Daedalus* who
makes them walk, when you're far more skilled than

Daedalus yourself at making them go round in a circle? 10
Don't you notice that our account has come full circle
back to the same point? You recall, no doubt, how we c
found earlier that what is holy and what is loved-by-
the-gods were not the same, but different from each
other? Don't you remember?

EUTHYPHRO. Yes, I do.

SOCRATES. Then don't you realize that now you're equat- 5
ing holy with what the gods love? But that makes it
identical with loved-by-the-gods, doesn't it?*

EUTHYPHRO. Indeed.

SOCRATES. So either our recent agreement wasn't sound;
or else, if it was, our present suggestion is wrong.

EUTHYPHRO. So it appears. 10

SOCRATES. Then we must start over again, and consider
what the holy is, since I shan't be willing to give up the
search till I learn the answer. Please don't scorn me, but d
give the matter your very closest attention and tell me
the truth—because you must know it, if any man does;
and like Proteus* you mustn't be let go until you tell it.

You see, if you didn't know for sure what is holy and
what unholy, there's no way you'd ever have ventured 5
to prosecute your elderly father for murder on behalf of
a labourer. Instead, fear of the gods would have saved
you from the risk of acting wrongly, and you'd have been
embarrassed in front of human beings.* But in fact I'm
quite sure that you think you have certain knowledge of e
what is holy and what is not; so tell me what you believe
it to be, excellent Euthyphro, and don't conceal it.

EUTHYPHRO. Some other time, Socrates: I'm hurrying some-
where just now, and it's time for me to be off.

SOCRATES. What a way to behave, my friend, going off 5
like this, and dashing the high hopes I held! I was hop-
ing I'd learn from you what acts are holy and what are
not, and so escape Meletus' indictment, by showing him
that Euthyphro had made me an expert in religion, and 16a
that my ignorance no longer made me a free-thinker or
innovator on that subject: and also, of course, that I
would live better for what remains of my life.*

DEFENCE OF SOCRATES

DEFENCE OF SOCRATES

I don't know* how you, fellow Athenians,* have been 17a
affected by my accusers, but for my part I felt myself
almost transported by them, so persuasively did they
speak. And yet hardly a word they have said is true. Among
their many falsehoods, one especially astonished me: their   5
warning that you must† be careful not to be taken in by
me, because I am a clever speaker. It seemed to me the   b
height of impudence on their part not to be embarrassed
at being refuted straight away by the facts, once it became
apparent that I was not a clever speaker at all—unless
indeed they call a 'clever' speaker one who speaks the   5
truth. If that is what they mean, then I would admit to
being an orator, although not on a par with them.

As I said, then, my accusers have said little or nothing
true; whereas from me you shall hear the whole truth,
though not, I assure you, fellow Athenians, in language
adorned with fine words and phrases or dressed up, as   c
theirs was: you shall hear my points made spontaneously
in whatever words occur to me—persuaded as I am that
my case is just. None of you should expect anything to be
put differently, because it would not, of course, be at all
fitting at my age, gentlemen, to come before you with   5
artificial speeches, such as might be composed by a young
lad.

One thing, moreover, I would earnestly beg of you,
fellow Athenians. If you hear me defending myself with
the same arguments I normally use at the bankers' tables
in the market-place (where many of you have heard me)   10
and elsewhere, please do not be surprised or protest on   d
that account. You see, here is the reason: this is the first
time I have ever appeared before a court of law, although
I am over 70; so I am literally a stranger to the diction of
this place. And if I really were a foreigner, you would naturally excuse me, were I to speak in the dialect and style   5
in which I had been brought up; so in the present case as   18a

27

well I ask you, in all fairness as I think, to disregard my manner of speaking—it may not be as good, or it may be better—but to consider and attend simply to the question whether or not my case is just; because that is the duty of a judge, as it is an orator's duty to speak the truth.

To begin with, fellow Athenians, it is fair that I should defend myself against the first set of charges falsely brought against me by my first accusers, and then turn to the later charges and the more recent ones. You see, I have been accused before you by many people for a long time now, for many years in fact, by people who spoke not a word of truth. It is those people I fear more than Anytus and his crowd, though they too are dangerous. But those others are more so, gentlemen: they have taken hold of most of you since childhood, and made persuasive accusations against me, yet without an ounce more truth in them. They say that there is one Socrates, a 'wise man',* who ponders what is above the earth and investigates everything beneath it, and turns the weaker argument into the stronger.*

Those accusers who have spread such rumour about me, fellow Athenians, are the dangerous ones, because their audience believes that people who inquire into those matters also fail to acknowledge the gods.* Moreover, those accusers are numerous, and have been denouncing me for a long time now, and they also spoke to you at an age at which you would be most likely to believe them, when some of you were children or young lads; and their accusations simply went by default for lack of any defence. But the most absurd thing of all is that one cannot even get to know their names or say who they were—except perhaps one who happens to be a comic playwright.* The ones who have persuaded you by malicious slander, and also some who persuade others because they have been persuaded themselves, are all very hard to deal with: one cannot put any of them on the stand here in court, or cross-examine anybody, but one must literally engage in a sort of shadow-boxing to defend oneself, and cross-examine without anyone to answer. You too, then, should allow, as I just said,

that I have two sets of accusers: one set who have accused
me recently, and the other of long standing to whom I   e
was just referring. And please grant that I need to defend
myself against the latter first, since you too heard them
accusing me earlier, and you heard far more from them
than from these recent critics here.

Very well, then. I must defend myself, fellow Athenians,   5
and in so short a time* must try to dispel the slander   19a
which you have had so long to absorb. That is the outcome I would wish for, should it be of any benefit to you
and to me, and I should like to succeed in my defence*—
though I believe the task to be a difficult one, and am well   5
aware of its nature. But let that turn out as God wills: I
have to obey the law* and present my defence.

   Let us examine, from the beginning, the charge that has
given rise to the slander against me—which was just what   b
Meletus relied upon when he drew up this indictment.
Very well then, what were my slanderers actually saying
when they slandered me? Let me read out their deposition, as if they were my legal accusers:

   'Socrates is guilty of being a busybody, in that he in-
quires into what is beneath the earth and in the sky, turns   5
the weaker argument into the stronger, and teaches others   c
to do the same.'

   The charges would run something like that. Indeed,
you can see them for yourselves, enacted in Aristophanes'
comedy: in that play, a character called 'Socrates' swings
around, claims to be walking on air,* and talks a lot of
other nonsense on subjects of which I have no under-   5
standing, great or small.

   Not that I mean to belittle knowledge of that sort, if
anyone really is learned in such matters—no matter how
many of Meletus' lawsuits I might have to defend myself
against—but the fact is, fellow Athenians, those subjects
are not my concern at all.* I call most of you to witness   d
yourselves, and I ask you to make that quite clear to one
another, if you have ever heard me in discussion (as many
of you have). Tell one another, then, whether any of you

5   has ever heard me discussing such subjects, either briefly or at length; and as a result you will realize that the other things said about me by the public are equally baseless.

In any event, there is no truth in those charges. Moreover, if you have heard from anyone that I undertake to

e   educate people and charge fees, there is no truth in that either—though for that matter I do think it also a fine thing if anyone *is* able to educate people, as Gorgias of Leontini, Prodicus of Ceos, and Hippias of Elis profess to.

5   Each of them can visit any city, gentlemen, and persuade its young people, who may associate free of charge with

20a   any of their own citizens they wish, to leave those associations, and to join with them instead, paying fees and being grateful into the bargain.

On that topic, there is at present another expert here, a gentleman from Paros; I heard of his visit, because I happened to run into a man who has spent more money on

5   sophists* than everyone else put together—Callias, the son of Hipponicus. So I questioned him, since he has two sons himself.

'Callias,' I said, 'if your two sons had been born as colts or calves, we could find and engage a tutor who could

b   make them both excel superbly in the required qualities— and he'd be some sort of expert in horse-rearing or agriculture. But seeing that they are actually human, whom do you intend to engage as their tutor? Who has knowledge of the required human and civic qualities? I ask,

5   because I assume you've given thought to the matter, having sons yourself. Is there such a person,' I asked, 'or not?'

'Certainly,' he replied.

'Who is he?' I said; 'Where does he come from, and what does he charge for tuition?'

'His name is Evenus, Socrates,' he replied; 'He comes from Paros, and he charges 5 minas.'*

I thought Evenus was to be congratulated, if he really

c   did possess that skill and imparted it for such a modest charge. I, at any rate, would certainly be giving myself fine airs and graces if I possessed that knowledge. But the fact is, fellow Athenians, I do not.

Now perhaps one of you will interject: 'Well then, Socrates, what is the difficulty in your case? What is the source of these slanders against you? If you are not engaged in something out of the ordinary, why ever has so much rumour and talk arisen about you? It would surely never have arisen, unless you were up to something different from most people. Tell us what it is, then, so that we don't jump to conclusions about you.'

That speaker makes a fair point, I think; and so I will try to show you just what it is that has earned me my reputation and notoriety. Please hear me out. Some of you will perhaps think I am joking, but I assure you that I shall be telling you the whole truth.

You see, fellow Athenians, I have gained this reputation on account of nothing but a certain sort of wisdom. And what sort of wisdom is that? It is a human kind of wisdom, perhaps, since it might just be true that I have wisdom of that sort. Maybe the people I just mentioned* possess wisdom of a superhuman kind; otherwise I cannot explain it. For my part, I certainly do not possess that knowledge; and whoever says I do is lying and speaking with a view to slandering me—

Now please do not protest, fellow Athenians, even if I should sound to you rather boastful. I am not myself the source of the story I am about to tell you, but I shall refer you to a trustworthy authority. As evidence of my wisdom, if such it actually be, and of its nature, I shall call to witness before you the god at Delphi.*

You remember Chaerephon, of course. He was a friend of mine from youth, and also a comrade in your party, who shared your recent exile and restoration.* You recall too what sort of man Chaerephon was, how impetuous he was in any undertaking. Well, on one occasion he actually went to the Delphic oracle, and had the audacity to put the following question to it—as I said, please do not make a disturbance, gentlemen—he went and asked if there was anyone wiser than myself; to which the Pythia responded* that there was no one. His brother here will testify to the court about that story, since Chaerephon himself is deceased.

b   Now keep in mind why I have been telling you this: it is because I am going to explain to you the origin of the slander against me. When I heard the story, I thought to myself: 'What ever is the god saying? What can his riddle mean?* Since I am all too conscious of not being wise in

5   any matter, great or small, what ever can he mean by pronouncing me to be the wisest? Surely he cannot be lying: for him that would be out of the question.'*

So for a long time I was perplexed about what he could possibly mean. But then, with great reluctance, I proceeded to investigate the matter somewhat as follows. I went to one of the people who had a reputation for wisdom, think-

c   ing there, if anywhere, to disprove the oracle's utterance and declare to it: 'Here is someone wiser than I am, and yet you said that I was the wisest.'

So I interviewed this person—I need not mention his name, but he was someone in public life; and when I examined him, my experience went something like this,

5   fellow Athenians: in conversing with him, I formed the opinion that, although the man was thought to be wise by many other people, and especially by himself, yet in reality he was not. So I then tried to show him that he thought

d   himself wise without being so. I thereby earned his dislike, and that of many people present; but still, as I went away, I thought to myself: 'I am wiser than that fellow, anyhow. Because neither of us, I dare say, knows anything of great

5   value; but he thinks he knows a thing when he doesn't; whereas I neither know it in fact, nor think that I do. At any rate, it appears that I am wiser than he in just this one small respect: if I do not know something, I do not think that I do.'

Next, I went to someone else, among people thought to be even wiser than the previous man, and I came to the

e   same conclusion again; and so I was disliked by that man too, as well as by many others.

Well, after that I went on to visit one person after another. I realized, with dismay and alarm, that I was making enemies; but even so, I thought it my duty to attach the highest importance to the god's business; and

therefore, in seeking the oracle's meaning, I had to go on   5
to examine all those with any reputation for knowledge.   22a
And upon my word,* fellow Athenians—because I am
obliged to speak the truth before the court—I truly did
experience something like this: as I pursued the god's inquiry, I found those held in the highest esteem were practically the most defective, whereas men who were supposed
to be their inferiors were much better off in respect of   5
understanding.

Let me, then, outline my wanderings for you, the various 'labours' I kept undertaking,* only to find that the
oracle proved completely irrefutable. After I had done with
the politicians, I turned to the poets—including tragedians,
dithyrambic poets,* and the rest—thinking that in their   b
company I would be shown up as more ignorant than
they were. So I picked up the poems over which I thought
they had taken the most trouble, and questioned them
about their meaning, so that I might also learn something   5
from them in the process.

Now I'm embarrassed to tell you the truth, gentlemen,
but it has to be said. Practically everyone else present
could speak better than the poets themselves about their
very own compositions. And so, once more, I soon realized this truth about them too:* it was not from wisdom
that they composed their works, but from a certain nat-   c
ural aptitude and inspiration, like that of seers and soothsayers*—because those people too utter many fine words,
yet know nothing of the matters on which they pronounce.
It was obvious to me that the poets were in much the
same situation; yet at the same time I realized that because   5
of their compositions they thought themselves the wisest
people in other matters as well, when they were not. So
I left, believing that I was ahead of them in the same way
as I was ahead of the politicians.

Then, finally, I went to the craftsmen, because I was
conscious of knowing almost nothing myself, but felt sure   d
that amongst them, at least, I would find much valuable
knowledge. And in that expectation I was not disappointed:
they did have knowledge in fields where I had none, and in

that respect they were wiser than I. And yet, fellow Athenians, those able craftsmen seemed to me to suffer from
the same failing as the poets: because of their excellence
at their own trade, each claimed to be a great expert also
on matters of the utmost importance; and this arrogance
of theirs seemed to eclipse their wisdom. So I began to ask
myself, on the oracle's behalf, whether I should prefer to
be as I am, neither wise as they are wise, nor ignorant as
they are ignorant, or to possess both their attributes; and
in reply, I told myself and the oracle that I was better off
as I was.

The effect of this questioning, fellow Athenians, was to
earn me much hostility of a very vexing and trying sort,
which has given rise to numerous slanders, including this
reputation I have for being 'wise'—because those present
on each occasion imagine me to be wise regarding the
matters on which I examine others. But in fact, gentlemen, it would appear that it is only the god who is truly
wise; and that he is saying to us, through this oracle, that
human wisdom is worth little or nothing.* It seems that
when he says 'Socrates', he makes use of my name, merely
taking me as an example—as if to say, 'The wisest amongst
you, human beings, is anyone like Socrates who has recognized that with respect to wisdom he is truly worthless.'

That is why, even to this day, I still go about seeking
out and searching into anyone I believe to be wise, citizen
or foreigner, in obedience to the god. Then, as soon as I
find that someone is not wise, I assist the god* by proving
that he is not. Because of this occupation, I have had no
time at all for any activity to speak of, either in public
affairs or in my family life; indeed, because of my service
to the god, I live in extreme poverty.

In addition, the young people who follow me around
of their own accord,† the ones who have plenty of leisure
because their parents are wealthiest, enjoy listening to
people being cross-examined. Often, too, they copy my example themselves, and so attempt to cross-examine others.
And I imagine that they find a great abundance of people
who suppose themselves to possess some knowledge, but

really know little or nothing. Consequently, the people they question are angry with me, though not with themselves, and say that there is a nasty pestilence abroad called 'Socrates', who is corrupting the young.

Then, when asked just what he is doing or teaching, they have nothing to say, because they have no idea what he does; yet, rather than seem at a loss, they resort to the stock charges against all who pursue intellectual inquiry, trotting out 'things in the sky and beneath the earth', 'failing to acknowledge the gods', and 'turning the weaker argument into the stronger'. They would, I imagine, be loath to admit the truth, which is that their pretensions to knowledge have been exposed, and they are totally ignorant. So because these people have reputations to protect, I suppose, and are also both passionate and numerous, and have been speaking about me in a vigorous and persuasive style, they have long been filling your ears with vicious slander. It is on the strength of all this that Meletus, along with Anytus and Lycon, has proceeded against me: Meletus is aggrieved for the poets, Anytus for the craftsmen and politicians, and Lycon for the orators.* And so, as I began by saying, I should be surprised if I could rid your minds of this slander in so short a time, when so much of it has accumulated.

There is the truth for you, fellow Athenians. I have spoken it without concealing anything from you, major or minor, and without glossing over anything. And yet I am virtually certain that it is my very candour that makes enemies for me—which goes to show that I am right: the slander against me is to that effect, and such is its explanation. And whether you look for one now or later, that is what you will find.

So much for my defence before you against the charges brought by my first group of accusers. Next, I shall try to defend myself against Meletus, good patriot that he claims to be, and against my more recent critics. So once again, as if they were a fresh set of accusers, let me in turn review their deposition. It runs something like this:

'Socrates is guilty of corrupting the young, and of failing to acknowledge the gods acknowledged by the city,
c   but introducing new spiritual beings* instead.'

Such is the charge: let us examine each item within it.

Meletus says, then, that I am guilty of corrupting the
5   young. Well I reply, fellow Athenians, that Meletus is
guilty of trifling in a serious matter, in that he brings
people to trial on frivolous grounds, and professes grave
concern about matters for which he has never cared at
all.* I shall now try to prove to you too that that is so.

10   Step forward, Meletus, and answer me. It is your chief
d   concern, is it not, that our younger people shall be as
good as possible?

—It is.

Very well, will you please tell the judges who influences
them for the better—because you must obviously know,
seeing that you care? Having discovered me, as you allege,
5   to be the one who is corrupting them, you bring me before the judges here and accuse me. So speak up, and tell
the court who has an improving influence.

You see, Meletus, you remain silent, and have no answer. Yet doesn't that strike you as shameful, and as proof
in itself of exactly what I say—that you have never cared
about these matters at all? Come then, good fellow, tell us
10   who influences them for the better.

—The laws.

e   Yes, but that is not what I'm asking, excellent fellow.
I mean, which *person*, who already knows the laws to
begin with?

—These gentlemen, the judges, Socrates.

What are you saying, Meletus? Can these people edu-
5   cate the young, and do they have an improving influence?

—Most certainly.

All of them, or some but not others?

—All of them.

My goodness, what welcome news, and what a generous
supply of benefactors you speak of! And how about the
10   audience here in court? Do they too have an improving
25a   influence, or not?

—Yes, they do too.

And how about members of the Council?*

—Yes, the Councillors too.

But in that case, how about people in the Assembly, its   5
individual members, Meletus? They won't be corrupting
their youngers, will they? Won't they all be good influences as well?

—Yes, they will too.

So every person in Athens, it would appear, has an
excellent influence on them except for me, whereas I alone   10
am corrupting them. Is that what you're saying?

—That is emphatically what I'm saying.

Then I find myself, if we are to believe you, in a most
awkward predicament. Now answer me this. Do you
think the same is true of horses? Is it everybody who   b
improves them, while a single person spoils them? Or isn't
the opposite true: a single person, or at least very few
people, namely the horse-trainers, can improve them;
while lay people spoil them,* don't they, if they have to
do with horses and make use of them? Isn't that true of
horses as of all other animals, Meletus? Of course it is,   5
whether you and Anytus deny it or not. In fact, I dare
say our young people are extremely lucky if only one person is corrupting them, while everyone else is doing them   c
good.

All right, Meletus. Enough has been said to prove that
you never were concerned about the young. You betray
your irresponsibility plainly, because you have not cared
at all about the charges on which you bring me before this
court.

Furthermore, Meletus, tell us, in God's name, whether   5
it is better to live among good fellow citizens or bad ones.
Come sir, answer: I am not asking a hard question. Bad
people have a harmful impact upon their closest companions at any given time, don't they, whereas good people
have a good one?

—Yes.   10

Well, is there anyone who wants to be harmed by his   d
companions rather than benefited?—Be a good fellow and

keep on answering, as the law requires you to. Is there anyone who wants to be harmed?

5   —Of course not.

Now tell me this. In bringing me here, do you claim that I am corrupting and depraving the young intentionally or unintentionally?

—Intentionally, so I maintain.

Really, Meletus? Are you so much smarter at your age
10   than I at mine as to realize that the bad have a harmful impact upon their closest companions at any given time,
e   whereas the good have a beneficial effect? Am I, by contrast, so far gone in my stupidity as not to realize that if I make one of my companions vicious, I risk incurring harm at his hands? And am I, therefore, as you allege, doing so much damage intentionally?

5   That I cannot accept from you, Meletus, and neither could anyone else, I imagine. Either I am not corrupting
26a them—or if I am, I am doing so unintentionally;* so either way your charge is false. But if I am corrupting them unintentionally, the law does not require me to be brought to court for such mistakes, but rather to be taken aside for private instruction and admonition—since I shall obviously stop doing unintentional damage, if I learn better.
5   But you avoided association with me and were unwilling to instruct me. Instead you bring me to court, where the law requires you to bring people who need punishment rather than enlightenment.

Very well, fellow Athenians. That part of my case is
b   now proven: Meletus never cared about these matters, either a lot or a little. Nevertheless, Meletus, please tell us in what way you claim that I am corrupting our younger people. That is quite obvious, isn't it, from the indictment you drew up? It is by teaching them not to acknowledge the gods acknowledged by the city, but to accept new
5   spiritual beings instead? You mean, don't you, that I am corrupting them by teaching them that?*

—I most emphatically do.

Then, Meletus, in the name of those very gods we are now discussing, please clarify the matter further for me,

and for the jury here. You see, I cannot make out what   c
you mean. Is it that I am teaching people to acknowledge
that some gods exist—in which case it follows that I do
acknowledge their existence myself as well, and am not a
complete atheist, hence am not guilty on that count—and
yet that those gods are not the ones acknowledged by the
city, but different ones? Is that your charge against me—   5
namely, that they are different? Or are you saying that I
acknowledge no gods at all myself, and teach the same to
others?

—I am saying the latter: you acknowledge no gods at all.

What ever makes you say that, Meletus, you strange   d
fellow? Do I not even acknowledge, then, with the rest of
mankind, that the sun and the moon are gods?*

—By God, he does not, members of the jury, since he
claims that the sun is made of rock, and the moon of earth!   5

My dear Meletus, do you imagine that it is Anaxagoras
you are accusing?* Do you have such contempt for the
jury, and imagine them so illiterate as not to know that
books by Anaxagoras of Clazomenae are crammed with
such assertions? What's more, are the young learning   10
those things from me when they can acquire them at the   e
bookstalls,* now and then, for a drachma at most, and
so ridicule Socrates if he claims those ideas for his own,
especially when they are so bizarre? In God's name, do you
really think me as crazy as that? Do I acknowledge the
existence of no god at all?

—By God no, none whatever.   5

I can't believe you, Meletus—nor, I think, can you believe yourself. To my mind, fellow Athenians, this fellow
is an impudent scoundrel who has framed this indictment
out of sheer wanton impudence and insolence. He seems to   27a
have devised a sort of riddle in order to try me out: 'Will
Socrates the Wise tumble to my nice self-contradiction?*
Or shall I fool him along with my other listeners?' You
see, he seems to me to be contradicting himself in the   5
indictment. It's as if he were saying: 'Socrates is guilty of
not acknowledging gods, but of acknowledging gods'; and
yet that is sheer tomfoolery.

I ask you to examine with me, gentlemen, just how that
10 appears to be his meaning. Answer for us, Meletus; and
b the rest of you, please remember my initial request not to
protest if I conduct the argument in my usual manner.*

Is there anyone in the world, Meletus, who acknowledges that human phenomena exist, yet does not acknowledge human beings?—Require him to answer, gentlemen,
5 and not to raise all kinds of confused objections. Is there
anyone who does not acknowledge horses, yet does acknowledge equestrian phenomena? Or who does not acknowledge that musicians exist, yet does acknowledge
musical phenomena?*

There is no one, excellent fellow: if you don't wish to
answer, I must answer for you, and for the jurors here.
c But at least answer my next question yourself. Is there
anyone who acknowledges that spiritual phenomena exist,
yet does not acknowledge spirits?
—No.

How good of you to answer—albeit reluctantly and
under compulsion from the jury. Well now, you say that
5 I acknowledge spiritual beings* and teach others to do so.
Whether they actually be new or old is no matter: I do at
any rate, by your account, acknowledge spiritual beings,
which you have also mentioned in your sworn deposition. But if I acknowledge spiritual beings, then surely it
follows quite inevitably that I must acknowledge spirits.
10 Is that not so?—Yes, it is so: I assume your agreement,
d since you don't answer. But we regard spirits, don't we,
as either gods or children of gods? Yes or no?
—Yes.

Then given that I do believe in spirits, as you say, if
5 spirits are gods of some sort, this is precisely what I claim
when I say that you are presenting us with a riddle and
making fun of us: you are saying that I do not believe in
gods, and yet again that I do believe in gods, seeing that
I believe in spirits.

On the other hand, if spirits are children of gods,* some
sort of bastard offspring from nymphs—or from whomever they are traditionally said, in each case, to be born

—then who in the world could ever believe that there   10
were children of gods, yet no gods? That would be just as   e
absurd as accepting the existence of children of horses and
asses[†]—namely, mules—yet rejecting the existence of horses
or asses!

In short, Meletus, you can only have drafted this[†] either
by way of trying us out, or because you were at a loss
how to charge me with a genuine offence. How could you   5
possibly persuade anyone with even the slightest intelligence that someone who accepts spiritual beings does not
also accept divine ones,[†] and again that the same person
also accepts neither spirits nor gods nor heroes? There is   28a
no conceivable way.

But enough, fellow Athenians. It needs no long defence,
I think, to show that I am not guilty of the charges in
Meletus' indictment; the foregoing will suffice. You may   5
be sure, though, that what I was saying earlier is true: I
have earned great hostility among many people. And that
is what will convict me, if I am convicted: not Meletus or
Anytus, but the slander and malice of the crowd. They
have certainly convicted many other good men as well,   b
and I imagine they will do so again; there is no risk of
their stopping with me.

Now someone may perhaps say: 'Well then, are you not
ashamed, Socrates, to have pursued a way of life which
has now put you at risk of death?'

But it may be fair for me to answer him as follows: 5
'You are sadly mistaken, fellow, if you suppose that a
man with even a grain of self-respect should reckon up
the risks of living or dying, rather than simply consider,
whenever he does something, whether his actions are just
or unjust, the deeds of a good man or a bad one. By your   c
principles, presumably, all those demigods who died in
the plain of Troy* were inferior creatures—yes, even the
son of Thetis,* who showed so much scorn for danger,
when the alternative was to endure dishonour. Thus, when
he was eager to slay Hector, his mother, goddess that she   5
was, spoke to him—something like this, I fancy:

41

> My child, if thou dost avenge the murder of thy friend, Patroclus,
> And dost slay Hector, then straightway [so runs the poem]
> Shalt thou die thyself, since doom is prepared for thee
> Next after Hector's.

10
d
But though he heard that, he made light of death and danger, since he feared far more to live as a base man, and to fail to avenge his dear ones. The poem goes on:

> Then straightway let me die, once I have given the wrongdoer
> His deserts, lest I remain here by the beak-prowed ships,
> An object of derision, and a burden upon the earth.

Can you suppose that he gave any thought to death or danger?

5
You see, here is the truth of the matter, fellow Athenians. Wherever a man has taken up a position because he considers it best, or has been posted there by his commander, that is where I believe he should remain, steadfast in danger, taking no account at all of death or of anything else rather than dishonour. I would therefore
e
have been acting absurdly, fellow Athenians, if when assigned to a post at Potidaea, Amphipolis, or Delium* by the superiors you had elected to command me, I remained where I was posted on those occasions at the risk of death, if ever any man did; whereas now that the god assigns me,
5
as I became completely convinced, to the duty of leading the philosophical life by examining myself and others, I
29a
desert that post from fear of death or anything else. Yes, that would be unthinkable; and then I truly should deserve to be brought to court for failing to acknowledge the gods' existence, in that I was disobedient to the oracle, was afraid of death, and thought I was wise when I was not.
5
After all, gentlemen, the fear of death amounts simply to thinking one is wise when one is not: it is thinking one knows something one does not know. No one knows, you see, whether death may not in fact prove the greatest of all blessings for mankind; but people fear it as if they
b
knew it for certain to be the greatest of evils. And yet† to think that one knows what one does not know must surely be the kind of folly which is reprehensible.

On this matter especially, gentlemen, that may be the nature of my own advantage over most people. If I really were to claim to be wiser than anyone in any respect, it would consist simply in this: just as I do not possess adequate knowledge of life in Hades,* so I also realize that   5
I do not possess it; whereas acting unjustly in disobedience to one's betters, whether god or human being, is something I *know* to be evil and shameful. Hence I shall never fear or flee from something which may indeed be a good for all I know, rather than from things I know to be evils.

Suppose, therefore, that you pay no heed to Anytus, but   c
are prepared to let me go. He said I need never have been brought to court in the first place; but that once I had been, your only option was to put me to death.* He declared before you that, if I got away from you this time, your sons would all be utterly corrupted by practising   5
Socrates' teachings. Suppose, in the face of that, you were to say to me:

'Socrates, we will not listen to Anytus this time. We are prepared to let you go—but only on this condition: you are to pursue that quest of yours and practise philosophy no longer; and if you are caught doing it any more, you shall be put to death.'

Well, as I just said, if you were prepared to let me go   d
on those terms, I should reply to you as follows:

'I have the greatest fondness and affection for you, fellow Athenians, but I will obey my god rather than you; and so long as I draw breath and am able, I shall never give up practising philosophy, or exhorting and showing   5
the way to any of you whom I ever encounter, by giving my usual sort of message. "Excellent friend," I shall say; "You are an Athenian. Your city is the most important and renowned for its wisdom and power; so are you not ashamed that, while you take care to acquire as much wealth as possible, with honour and glory as well, yet you   e
take no care or thought for understanding or truth, or for the best possible state of your soul?"'

'And should any of you dispute that, and claim that he

43

does take such care, I will not let him go straight away
5   nor leave him, but I will question and examine and put
30a   him to the test; and if I do not think he has acquired
goodness, though he says he has, I shall say, "Shame on
you, for setting the lowest value upon the most precious
things, and for rating inferior ones more highly!" That I
shall do for anyone I encounter, young or old, alien or
fellow citizen; but all the more for the latter, since your
5   kinship with me is closer.'

Those are my orders from my god, I do assure you.
Indeed, I believe that no greater good has ever befallen you
in our city than my service to my god; because all I do is
to go about persuading you, young and old alike, not to
b   care for your bodies or for your wealth so intensely as for
the greatest possible well-being of your souls. 'It is not
wealth', I tell you, 'that produces goodness; rather, it is
from goodness that wealth, and all other benefits for human
beings, accrue to them in their private and public life.'*

5   If, in fact, I am corrupting the young by those assertions, you may call them harmful. But if anyone claims
that I say anything different, he is talking nonsense. In the
face of that I should like to say: 'Fellow Athenians, you
may listen to Anytus or not, as you please; and you may
let me go or not, as you please, because there is no chance
c   of my acting otherwise, even if I have to die many times
over—'

Stop protesting, fellow Athenians! Please abide by my
request* that you not protest against what I say, but hear
5   me out; in fact, it will be in your interest, so I believe, to
do so. You see, I am going to say some further things to
you which may make you shout out—although I beg you
not to.

You may be assured that if you put to death the sort of
man I just said I was, you will not harm me more than
10   you harm yourselves. Meletus or Anytus would not harm
me at all; nor, in fact, could they do so, since I believe it is
d   out of the question for a better man to be harmed by his
inferior. The latter may, of course, inflict death or banishment or disenfranchisement; and my accuser here, along

with others no doubt, believes those to be great evils. But
I do not. Rather, I believe it a far greater evil to try to kill   5
a man unjustly, as he does now.

At this point, therefore, fellow Athenians, so far from
pleading on my own behalf, as might be supposed, I am
pleading on yours, in case by condemning me you should
mistreat the gift which God has bestowed upon you—
because if you put me to death, you will not easily find   e
another like me. The fact is, if I may put the point in a
somewhat comical way, that I have been literally attached
by God to our city, as if to a horse—a large thorough-
bred, which is a bit sluggish because of its size, and needs   5
to be aroused by some sort of gadfly. Yes, in me, I believe,
God has attached to our city just such a creature—the
kind which is constantly alighting everywhere on you,   31a
all day long, arousing, cajoling, or reproaching each and
every one of you. You will not easily acquire another such
gadfly, gentlemen; rather, if you take my advice, you will
spare my life. I dare say, though, that you will get angry,
like people who are awakened from their doze. Perhaps
you will heed Anytus, and give me a swat: you could hap-   5
pily finish me off, and then spend the rest of your life
asleep—unless God, in his compassion for you, were to
send you someone else.

That I am, in fact, just the sort of gift that God would
send to our city, you may recognize from this: it would
not seem to be in human nature* for me to have neglected   b
all my own affairs, and put up with the neglect of my
family for all these years, but constantly minded your
interests, by visiting each of you in private like a father or
an elder brother, urging you to be concerned about good-   5
ness. Of course, if I were gaining anything from that, or
were being paid to urge that course upon you, my actions
could be explained. But in fact you can see for yourselves
that my accusers, who so shamelessly level all those other
charges against me, could not muster the impudence to
call evidence that I ever once obtained payment, or asked   c
for any. It is I who can call evidence sufficient, I think, to
show that I am speaking the truth—namely, my poverty.

Now it may perhaps seem peculiar that, as some say, I
5   give this counsel by going around and dealing with others'
concerns in private, yet do not venture to appear before
the Assembly, and counsel the city about your business in
public. But the reason for that is one you have frequently
d   heard me give in many places: it is a certain divine or
spiritual sign* which comes to me, the very thing to which
Meletus made mocking allusion in his indictment. It has
been happening to me ever since childhood: a voice of
some sort which comes, and which always—whenever it
does come—restrains me from what I am about to do, yet
5   never gives positive direction. That is what opposes my
engaging in politics—and its opposition is an excellent
thing, to my mind; because you may be quite sure, fellow
Athenians, that if I had tried to engage in politics,† I should
e   have perished long since, and should have been of no use
either to you or to myself.

And please do not get angry if I tell you the truth. The
fact is that there is no person on earth whose life will be
spared by you or by any other majority, if he is genuinely
opposed to many injustices and unlawful acts, and tries to
32a prevent their occurrence in our city. Rather, anyone who
truly fights for what is just, if he is going to survive for
even a short time, must act in a private capacity rather
than a public one.

I will offer you conclusive evidence of that—not just
5   words, but the sort of evidence that you respect, namely,
actions. Just hear me tell my experiences, so that you may
know that I would not submit to a single person for fear
of death, contrary to what is just; nor would I do so, even
if I were to lose my life on the spot. I shall mention things
to you which are vulgar commonplaces of the courts; yet
they are true.

b   Although I have never held any other public office in
our city, fellow Athenians, I have served on its Council.
My own tribe, Antiochis, happened to be the presiding
commission* on the occasion when you wanted† a collective trial for the ten generals who had failed to rescue the
survivors from the naval battle.* That was illegal, as you

all later recognized. At the time I was the only commis-   5
sioner opposed to your acting illegally, and I voted against
the motion. And though its advocates were prepared to
lay information against me and have me arrested, while
you were urging them on by shouting, I believed that I   c
should face danger in siding with law and justice, rather
than take your side for fear of imprisonment or death,
when your proposals were contrary to justice.

Those events took place while our city was still under
democratic rule. But on a subsequent occasion, after the
oligarchy had come to power, the Thirty* summoned me
and four others to the round chamber,* with orders to   5
arrest Leon the Salaminian, and fetch him from Salamis*
for execution; they were constantly issuing such orders, of
course, to many others, in their wish to implicate as many
as possible in their crimes. On that occasion, however, I
showed, once again not just by words, but by my actions,   d
that I couldn't care less about death—if that would not be
putting it rather crudely—but that my one and only care
was to avoid doing anything sinful or unjust. Thus, powerful as it was, that regime did not frighten me into unjust
action: when we emerged from the round chamber, the   5
other four went off to Salamis and arrested Leon, whereas
I left them and went off home. For that I might easily
have been put to death, had the regime not collapsed
shortly afterwards. There are many witnesses who will   e
testify before you about those events.

Do you imagine, then, that I would have survived all
these years if I had been regularly active in public life,
and had championed what was right in a manner worthy
of a brave man, and valued that above all else, as was
my duty? Far from it, fellow Athenians: I would not, and   5
nor would any other man. But in any public undertaking,   33a
that is the sort of person that I, for my part, shall prove
to have been throughout my life; and likewise in my private life, because I have never been guilty of unjust association with anyone, including those whom my slanderers
allege to have been my students.*   5

I never, in fact, was anyone's instructor* at any time.

47

But if a person wanted to hear me talking, while I was engaging in my own business, I never grudged that to anyone, young or old; nor do I hold conversation only

b   when I receive payment, and not otherwise. Rather, I offer myself for questioning to wealthy and poor alike, and to anyone who may wish to answer in response to questions from me. Whether any of those people acquires a good

5   character or not, I cannot fairly be held responsible, when I never at any time promised any of them that they would learn anything from me, nor gave them instruction. And if anyone claims that he ever learnt anything from me, or has heard privately something that everyone else did not hear as well, you may be sure that what he says is untrue.

Why then, you may ask, do some people enjoy spending so much time in my company? You have already heard,

c   fellow Athenians: I have told you the whole truth—which is that my listeners enjoy the examination of those who think themselves wise but are not, since the process is not unamusing. But for me, I must tell you, it is a mission

5   which I have been bidden to undertake by the god, through oracles and dreams,* and through every means whereby a divine injunction to perform any task has ever been laid upon a human being.*

That is not only true, fellow Athenians, but is easily

d   verified—because if I do corrupt any of our young people, or have corrupted others in the past, then presumably, when they grew older, should any of them have realized that I had at any time given them bad advice in their youth, they ought now to have appeared here themselves

5   to accuse me and obtain redress. Or else, if they were unwilling to come in person, members of their families— fathers, brothers, or other relations—had their relatives suffered any harm at my hands, ought now to put it on record and obtain redress.

10   In any case, many of those people are present, whom I

e   can see: first there is Crito, my contemporary and fellow demesman, father of Critobulus here; then Lysanias of Sphettus, father of Aeschines here; next, Epigenes' father, Antiphon from Cephisia, is present; then again, there are

48

others here whose brothers have spent time with me in
these studies: Nicostratus, son of Theozotides, brother of
Theodotus—Theodotus himself, incidentally, is deceased,   5
so Nicostratus could not have come at his brother's urging; and Paralius here, son of Demodocus, whose brother
was Theages; also present is Ariston's son, Adimantus,   34a
whose brother is Plato here;* and Aeantodorus, whose
brother is Apollodorus here.

There are many others I could mention to you, from
whom Meletus should surely have called some testimony
during his own speech. However, if he forgot to do so   5
then, let him call it now—I yield the floor to him—and if
he has any such evidence, let him produce it. But quite the
opposite is true, gentlemen: you will find that they are all
prepared to support me, their corruptor, the one who is,
according to Meletus and Anytus, doing their relatives
mischief. Support for me from the actual victims of cor-   b
ruption might perhaps be explained; but what of the
uncorrupted—older men by now, and relatives of my victims? What reason would they have to support me, apart
from the right and proper one, which is that they know
very well that Meletus is lying, whereas I am telling the   5
truth?

There it is, then, gentlemen. That, and perhaps more of
the same, is about all I have to say in my defence. But
perhaps, among your number, there may be someone
who will harbour resentment when he recalls a case of his   c
own: he may have faced a less serious trial than this one,
yet begged and implored the jury, weeping copiously,
and producing his children here, along with many other
relatives and loved ones, to gain as much sympathy as pos-   5
sible. By contrast, I shall do none of those things, even
though I am running what might be considered the ultimate risk. Perhaps someone with those thoughts will harden
his heart against me; and enraged by those same thoughts,
he may cast his vote against me in anger. Well, if any of   d
you are so inclined—not that I expect it of you, but if anyone *should* be—I think it fair to answer him as follows:

49

'I naturally do have relatives, my excellent friend, because—in Homer's own words*—I too was "not born of
5 oak nor of rock", but of human parents; and so I do have
relatives—including my sons,* fellow Athenians. There are
three of them: one is now a youth, while two are still
children. Nevertheless, I shall not produce any of them
here, and then entreat you to vote for my acquittal.'

10 And why, you may ask, will I do no such thing? Not
e out of contempt or disrespect for you, fellow Athenians—
whether or not I am facing death boldly is a different
issue. The point is that with our reputations in mind—
yours and our whole city's, as well as my own—I believe
that any such behaviour would be ignominious, at my age
and with the reputation I possess; that reputation may or
5 may not, in fact, be deserved, but at least it is believed
35a that Socrates stands out in some way from the run of
human beings. Well, if those of you who are believed to
be pre-eminent in wisdom, courage, or any other form
of goodness, are going to behave like that, it would be
demeaning.

I have frequently seen such men when they face judgment: they have significant reputations, yet they put on
5 astonishing performances, apparently in the belief that by
dying they will suffer something unheard of—as if they
would be immune from death, so long as you did not kill
them! They seem to me to put our city to shame: they
b could give any foreigner the impression that men pre-
eminent among Athenians in goodness, whom they select
from their own number to govern and hold other positions, are no better than women.* I say this, fellow Athenians, because none of us† who has even the slightest
5 reputation should behave like that; nor should you put up
with us if we try to do so. Rather, you should make one
thing clear: you will be far more inclined to convict one
who stages those pathetic charades and makes our city an
object of derision, than one who keeps his composure.

10 But leaving reputation aside, gentlemen, I do not think
c it right to entreat the jury, nor to win acquittal in that
way, instead of by informing and persuading them. A

juror does not sit to dispense justice as a favour, but to
determine where it lies. And he has sworn, not that he will
favour whomever he pleases, but that he will try the case
according to law. We should not, then, accustom you to   5
transgress your oath, nor should you become accustomed
to doing so: neither of us would be showing respect towards the gods. And therefore, fellow Athenians, do not
require behaviour from me towards you which I consider   d
neither proper nor right nor pious—more especially now,
for God's sake, when I stand charged by Meletus here
with impiety: because if I tried to persuade and coerce
you with entreaties in spite of your oath, I clearly *would*
be teaching you not to believe in gods; and I would stand   5
literally self-convicted, by my defence, of failing to acknowledge them. But that is far from the truth: I do acknowledge them, fellow Athenians, as none of my accusers do;*
and I trust to you, and to God, to judge my case as shall
be best for me and for yourselves.

*

For many reasons, fellow Athenians, I am not dismayed   e
by this outcome[1]—your convicting me, I mean—and espe-   36a
cially because the outcome has come as no surprise to me.
I wonder far more at the number of votes cast on each
side, because I did not think the margin would be so
narrow. Yet it seems, in fact, that if a mere thirty votes   5
had gone the other way, I should have been acquitted.*
Or rather, even as things stand, I consider that I have been
cleared of Meletus' charges. Not only that, but one thing
is obvious to everyone: if Anytus had not come forward
with Lycon to accuse me, Meletus would have forfeited
1,000 drachmas, since he would not have gained one-fifth   b
of the votes cast.*

But anyhow, this gentleman demands the death penalty
for me. Very well, then: what alternative penalty* shall I
suggest to you, fellow Athenians? Clearly, it must be one
I deserve. So what do I deserve to incur or to pay, for   5

---

[1] The verdict was 'Guilty'. Socrates here begins his second speech, proposing an alternative to the death penalty demanded by the prosecution.

having taken it into my head not to lead an inactive life? Instead, I have neglected the things that concern most people—making money, managing an estate, gaining military or civic honours, or other positions of power, or joining political clubs and parties which have formed in our

c   city. I thought myself, in truth, too honest to survive if I engaged in those things. I did not pursue a course, therefore, in which I would be of no use to you or to myself. Instead, by going to each individual privately, I tried to render a service for you which is—so I maintain—the highest

5   service of all. Therefore that was the course I followed: I tried to persuade each of you not to care for any of his possessions rather than care for himself, striving for the utmost excellence and understanding; and not to care for our city's possessions rather than for the city itself; and to

d   care about other things in the same way.

So what treatment do I deserve for being such a benefactor? If I am to make a proposal truly in keeping with my deserts, fellow Athenians, it should be some benefit; and moreover, the sort of benefit that would be fitting

5   for me. Well then, what *is* fitting for a poor man who is a benefactor, and who needs time free for exhorting you? Nothing could be more fitting,† fellow Athenians, than to give such a man regular free meals in the Prytaneum;* indeed, that is far more fitting for him than for any of you who may have won an Olympic race with a pair or a team of horses: that victor brings you only the appearance

10   of success, whereas I bring you the reality; besides, he is
e   not in want of sustenance, whereas I am. So if, as justice
37a demands, I am to make a proposal in keeping with my deserts, that is what I suggest: free meals in the Prytaneum.

Now, in proposing this, I may seem to you, as when I talked about appeals for sympathy, to be speaking from

5   sheer effrontery. But actually I have no such motive, fellow Athenians. My point is rather this: I am convinced that I do not treat any human being unjustly, at least intentionally*—but I cannot make you share that conviction, because we have conversed together so briefly. I say this, because if it were the law here, as in other jurisdictions,

that a capital case must not be tried in a single day, but   10
over several,* I think you could have been convinced; but   b
as things stand, it is not easy to clear oneself of such grave
allegations in a short time.

Since, therefore, I am persuaded, for my part, that I
have treated no one unjustly, I have no intention whatever
of so treating myself, nor of denouncing myself as deserving ill, or proposing any such treatment for myself. Why   5
should I do that? For fear of the penalty Meletus demands
for me, when I say that I don't know if that is a good
thing or a bad one?* In preference to that, am I then to
choose one of the things I know very well to be bad,
and demand that instead? Imprisonment, for instance?
Why should I live in prison, in servitude to the annually   c
appointed prison commissioners?* Well then, a fine, with
imprisonment until I pay? That would amount to what I
just mentioned, since I haven't the means to pay it.

Well then, should I propose banishment? Perhaps that
is what you would propose for me. Yet I must surely be   5
obsessed with survival, fellow Athenians, if I am so illo-
gical as that. You, my fellow citizens, were unable to put
up with my discourses and arguments, but they were so   d
irksome and odious to you that you now seek to be rid of
them. Could I not draw the inference, in that case, that
others will hardly take kindly to them? Far from it, fellow
Athenians. A fine life it would be for a person of my age
to go into exile, and spend his days continually exchan-   5
ging one city for another, and being repeatedly expelled—
because I know very well that wherever I go, the young
will come to hear me speaking, as they do here. And if I
repel them, they will expel me themselves, by persuading
their elders; while if I do not repel them, their fathers and   e
relatives will expel me on their account.*

Now, perhaps someone may say: 'Socrates, could you
not be so kind as to keep quiet and remain inactive, while
living in exile?' This is the hardest point of all of which   5
to convince some of you. Why? Because, if I tell you that
that would mean disobeying my god, and that is why I
cannot remain inactive, you will disbelieve me and think   38a

that I am practising a sly evasion.* Again, if I said that it really is the greatest benefit for a person to converse every day about goodness, and about the other subjects you have
5   heard me discussing when examining myself and others— and that an unexamined life is no life for a human being to live*—then you would believe me still less when I made those assertions. But the facts, gentlemen, are just as I claim them to be, though it is not easy to convince you of them. At the same time, I am not accustomed to think of
b   myself as deserving anything bad. If I had money, I would have proposed a fine of as much as I could afford: that would have done me no harm at all. But the fact is that I have none—unless you wish to fix the penalty at a sum
5   I could pay. I could afford to pay you 1 mina, I suppose, so I suggest a fine of that amount—

One moment, fellow Athenians. Plato here, along with Crito, Critobulus, and Apollodorus, is urging me to propose 30 minas,* and they are saying they will stand surety for that sum. So I propose a fine of that amount, and these
10 people shall be your sufficient guarantors of its payment.

*

c   For the sake of a slight gain in time, fellow Athenians, you will incur infamy and blame from those who would denigrate our city, for putting Socrates to death[1]—a 'wise man'—because those who wish to malign you will say I am wise, even if I am not; in any case, had you waited
5   only a short time, you would have obtained that outcome automatically. You can see, of course, that I am now well advanced in life, and death is not far off. I address that
d   not to all of you, but to those who condemned me to death;* and to those same people I would add something further.

Perhaps you imagine, gentlemen, that I have been convicted for lack of arguments of the sort I could have used to convince you, had I believed that I should do or say any-
5   thing* to gain acquittal. But that is far from true. I have

---

[1] The jury has now voted for the death penalty, and Socrates begins his final speech.

been convicted, not for lack of arguments, but for lack of
brazen impudence and willingness to address you in such
terms as you would most like to be addressed in—that is
to say, by weeping and wailing, and doing and saying much
else that I claim to be unworthy of me—the sorts of thing   e
that you are so used to hearing from others. But just as I
did not think during my defence that I should do anything
unworthy of a free man because I was in danger, so now
I have no regrets about defending myself as I did; I should
far rather present such a defence and die, than live by
defending myself in that other fashion.   5

In court, as in warfare, neither I nor anyone else should
contrive to escape death at any cost. On the battlefield   39a
too, it often becomes obvious that one could avoid death
by throwing down one's arms and flinging oneself upon
the mercy of one's pursuers. And in every sort of danger
there are many other means of escaping death, if one is   5
shameless enough to do or to say anything. I suggest that
it is not death that is hard to avoid, gentlemen, but wickedness is far harder, since it is fleeter of foot than death.* b
Thus, slow and elderly as I am, I have now been overtaken by the slower runner; while my accusers, adroit and
quick-witted as they are, have been overtaken by the faster,
which is wickedness. And so I take my leave, condemned
to death by your judgment, whereas they stand for ever con- 5
demned to depravity and injustice as judged by Truth.*
And just as I accept my penalty, so must they. Things
were bound to turn out this way, I suppose, and I imagine it is for the best.

In the next place, to those of you who voted against me,   c
I wish to utter a prophecy. Indeed, I have now reached a
point at which people are most given to prophesying—
that is, when they are on the point of death.* I warn you,
my executioners, that as soon as I am dead retribution
will come upon you*—far more severe, I swear, than the   5
sentence you have passed upon me. You have tried to kill
me for now, in the belief that you will be relieved from
giving an account of your lives. But in fact, I can tell
you, you will face just the opposite outcome. There will

d   be more critics to call you to account, people whom I
have restrained for the time being though you were unaware of my doing so. They will be all the harder on you
since they are younger, and you will rue it all the more—
because if you imagine that by putting people to death
you will prevent anyone from reviling you for not living
5   rightly, you are badly mistaken. That way of escape is
neither feasible nor honourable. Rather, the most honourable and easiest way is not the silencing of others, but
striving to make oneself as good a person as possible. So
with that prophecy to those of you who voted against me,
10   I take my leave.

e   As for those who voted for my acquittal, I should like
to discuss the outcome of this case while the officials are
occupied, and I am not yet on the way to the place where
I must die. Please bear with me, gentlemen, just for this
short time: there is no reason why we should not have a
5   word with one another while that is still permitted.

40a   Since I regard you as my friends, I am willing to show
you the significance of what has just befallen me. You see,
gentlemen of the jury—and in applying that term to you,
I probably use it correctly*—something wonderful has
just happened to me. Hitherto, the usual prophetic voice
5   from my spiritual sign was continually active, and frequently opposed me even on trivial matters, if I was about
to do anything amiss. But now something has befallen me,
as you can see for yourselves, which one certainly might
consider—and is generally held—to be the very worst of
b   evils. Yet the sign from God did not oppose me, either
when I left home this morning, or when I appeared here
in court, or at any point when I was about to say anything
during my speech; and yet in other discussions it has very
5   often stopped me in mid-sentence. This time, though, it
has not opposed me at any moment in anything I said or
did in this whole business.

Now, what do I take to be the explanation for that?
I will tell you: I suspect that what has befallen me is a
blessing, and that those of us who suppose death to be an
c   evil cannot be making a correct assumption. I have gained

every ground for that suspicion, because my usual sign could not have failed to oppose me, unless I were going to incur some good result.

And let us also reflect upon how good a reason there is to hope that death is a good thing. It is, you see, one or other of two things: either to be dead is to be non-existent, as it were, and a dead person has no awareness whatever of anything at all; or else, as we are told, the soul undergoes some sort of transformation, or exchanging of this present world for another. Now if there is, in fact, no awareness in death, but it is like sleep—the kind in which the sleeper does not even dream at all*—then death would be a marvellous gain. Why, imagine that someone had to pick the night in which he slept so soundly that he did not even dream, and to compare all the other nights and days of his life with that one; suppose he had to say, upon consideration, how many days or nights in his life he had spent better and more agreeably than that night; in that case, I think he would find them easy to count compared with his other days and nights—even if he were the Great King of Persia,* let alone an ordinary person. Well, if death is like that, then for my part I call it a gain; because on that assumption the whole of time would seem no longer than a single night.

On the other hand, if death is like taking a trip from here to another place, and if it is true, as we are told, that all of the dead do indeed exist in that other place, why then, gentlemen of the jury, what could be a greater blessing than that? If upon arriving in Hades, and being rid of these people who profess to be 'jurors', one is going to find those who are truly judges, and who are also said to sit in judgment there*—Minos, Rhadamanthys, Aeacus, Triptolemus, and all other demigods who were righteous in their own lives—would that be a disappointing journey?

Or again, what would any of you not give to share the company of Orpheus and Musaeus, of Hesiod and Homer? I say 'you,' since I personally would be willing to die many times over, if those tales are true. Why?

b   Because my own sojourn there would be wonderful, if I
could meet Palamedes, or Ajax, son of Telamon, or anyone else of old who met their death through an unjust
verdict. Whenever I met them, I could compare my own
experiences with theirs—which would be not unamusing,
5   I fancy—and best of all, I could spend time questioning
and probing people there, just as I do here, to find out who
among them is truly wise, and who thinks he is without
being so.

What would one not give, gentlemen of the jury, to be
c   able to question the leader of the great expedition against
Troy,* or Odysseus, or Sisyphus, or countless other men
and women* one could mention? Would it not be unspeak-
able good fortune to converse with them there, to mingle
with them and question them? At least that isn't a reason,
5   presumably, for people in that world to put you to death
—because amongst other ways in which people there are
more fortunate than those in our world, they have become
immune from death for the rest of time, if what we are
told is actually true.

Moreover, you too, gentlemen of the jury, should be of
good hope in the face of death, and fix your minds upon
d   this single truth: nothing can harm a good man, either
in life or in death; nor are his fortunes neglected by the
gods. In fact, what has befallen me has come about by no
mere accident; rather, it is clear to me that it was better
5   I should die now and be rid of my troubles.* That is also
the reason why the divine sign at no point turned me back;
and for my part, I bear those who condemned me, and my
accusers, no ill will at all—though, to be sure, it was not
with that intent that they were condemning and accusing
e   me, but with intent to harm me—and they are culpable
for that. Still, this much I ask of them.* When my sons
come of age, gentlemen, punish them: give them the same
sort of trouble that I used to give you, if you think they
5   care for money or anything else more than for goodness,
and if they think highly of themselves when they are of
no value. Reprove them, as I reproved you, for failing to
care for the things they should, and for thinking highly

of themselves when they are worthless. If you will do that, **42a**
then I shall have received my own just deserts from you,
as will my sons.

But enough. It is now time to leave—for me to die, and
for you to live—though which of us has the better destiny
is unclear to everyone, save only to God.*   5

CRITO

CRITO

SOCRATES. Why have you come at this hour, Crito? It's 43a still very early, isn't it?

CRITO. Yes, very.

SOCRATES. About what time?

CRITO. Just before daybreak.

SOCRATES. I'm surprised the prison-warder was willing to 5 answer the door.

CRITO. He knows me by now, Socrates, because I come and go here so often; and besides, I've done him a small favour.

SOCRATES. Have you just arrived, or have you been here for a while?

CRITO. For quite a while. 10

SOCRATES. Then why didn't you wake me up right away b instead of sitting by me in silence?

CRITO. Well *of course* I didn't wake you, Socrates! I only wish I weren't so sleepless and wretched myself. I've been marvelling all this time as I saw how peacefully 5 you were sleeping, and I deliberately kept from waking you, so that you could pass the time as peacefully as possible. I've often admired your disposition in the past, in fact all your life; but more than ever in your present plight, you bear it so easily and patiently.

SOCRATES. Well, Crito, it really would be tiresome for a 10 man of my age to get upset if the time has come when he must end his life.

CRITO. And yet others of your age, Socrates, are over- c taken by similar troubles, but their age brings them no relief from being upset at the fate which faces them.

SOCRATES. That's true. But tell me, why *have* you come so early?

CRITO. I bring painful news, Socrates—not painful for you, 5 I suppose, but painful and hard for me and all your friends—and hardest of all for me to bear, I think.

SOCRATES. What news is that? Is it that the ship has come back from Delos,* the one on whose return I must die? d

63

CRITO. Well no, it hasn't arrived yet, but I think it will get here today, judging from reports of people who've come from Sunium,* where they disembarked. That† makes it
5   obvious that it will get here today; and so tomorrow, Socrates, you will have to end your life.

SOCRATES. Well, may that be for the best, Crito. If it so please the gods, so be it. All the same, I don't think it will get here today.

44a CRITO. What makes you think that?

SOCRATES. I'll tell you. You see, I am to die on the day after the ship arrives, am I not?

CRITO. At least that's what the authorities say.

5   SOCRATES. Then I don't think it will get here on the day that is just dawning, but on the next one. I infer that from a certain dream I had in the night*—a short time ago, so it may be just as well that you didn't wake me.

CRITO. And what was your dream?

10   SOCRATES. I dreamt that a lovely, handsome woman ap-
b   proached me, robed in white. She called me and said: 'Socrates,

Thou shalt reach fertile Phthia upon the third day.'*

CRITO. What a curious dream, Socrates.

5   SOCRATES. Yet its meaning is clear, I think, Crito.

CRITO. All too clear, it would seem. But please, Socrates, my dear friend, there is still time to take my advice, and make your escape—because if you die, I shall suffer more than one misfortune: not only shall I lose such a friend as I'll never find again, but it will look to many
10   people, who hardly know you or me, as if I'd aban-
c   doned you—since I could have rescued you if I'd been willing to put up the money. And yet what could be more shameful than a reputation for valuing money more highly than friends? Most people won't believe that it was you who refused to leave this place yourself,
5   despite our urging you to do so.

SOCRATES. But why should we care so much, my good Crito, about what most people believe? All the most capable people, whom we should take more seriously,

will think the matter has been handled exactly as it has
been.

CRITO. Yet surely, Socrates, you can see that one must   d
heed popular opinion too. Your present plight shows by
itself that the populace can inflict not the least of evils,
but just about the worst, if someone has been slandered
in their presence.   5

SOCRATES. Ah Crito, if only the populace *could* inflict
the worst of evils! Then they would also be capable of
providing the greatest of goods, and a fine thing that
would be. But the fact is that they can do neither: they
are unable to give anyone understanding or lack of it,*
no matter what they do.   10

CRITO. Well, if you say so. But tell me this, Socrates: can   e
it be that you are worried for me and your other friends,
in case the blackmailers* give us trouble, if you escape,
for having smuggled you out of here? Are you worried
that we might be forced to forfeit all our property as   5
well, or pay heavy fines, or even incur some further penalty? If you're afraid of anything like that, put it out of   45a
your mind. In rescuing you we are surely justified in
taking that risk, or even worse if need be. Come on,
listen to me and do as I say.

SOCRATES. Yes, those risks do worry me, Crito—amongst
many others.   5

CRITO. Then put those fears aside—because no great
sum is needed to pay people who are willing to rescue
you and get you out of here. Besides, you can surely
see that those blackmailers are cheap, and it wouldn't
take much to buy them off. My own means are avail-   b
able to you and would be ample, I'm sure. Then again,
even if—out of concern on my behalf—you think you
shouldn't be spending my money, there are visitors here
who are ready to spend theirs. One of them, Simmias
from Thebes, has actually brought enough money for
this very purpose, while Cebes and quite a number of   5
others are also prepared to contribute. So, as I say, you
shouldn't hesitate to save yourself on account of those
fears.

   And don't let it trouble you, as you were saying in
court,* that you wouldn't know what to do with your-
c self if you went into exile. There will be people to welcome you anywhere else you may go: if you want to go
   to Thessaly,* I have friends there who will make much
   of you and give you safe refuge, so that no one from
5 anywhere in Thessaly will trouble you.
   Next, Socrates, I don't think that what you propose—
   giving yourself up, when you could be rescued—is even
   just. You are actually hastening to bring upon yourself
   just the sorts of thing which your enemies would hasten
   to bring upon you—indeed, they have done so—in their
   wish to destroy you.
10   What's more, I think you're betraying those sons of
d yours.* You will be deserting them, if you go off when
   you could be raising and educating them: as far as you're
   concerned, they will fare as best they may. In all likelihood, they'll meet the sort of fate which usually be-
   falls orphans once they've lost their parents. Surely, one
5 should either not have children at all, or else see the toil
   and trouble of their upbringing and education through
   to the end; yet you seem to me to prefer the easiest
   path. One should rather choose the path that a good
   and resolute man would choose, particularly if one professes to cultivate goodness* all one's life. Frankly, I'm
e ashamed for you and for us, your friends: it may appear
   that this whole predicament of yours has been handled
   with a certain feebleness on our part. What with the
   bringing of your case to court when that could have
   been avoided,* the actual conduct of the trial, and now,
5 to crown it all, this absurd outcome of the business, it
   may seem that the problem has eluded us through some
46a fault or feebleness on our part—in that we failed to save
   you, and you failed to save yourself, when that was quite
   possible and feasible, if we had been any use at all.
   Make sure, Socrates, that all this doesn't turn out
   badly, and a disgrace to you as well as us. Come now,
   form a plan—or rather, don't even plan, because the
5 time for that is past, and only a single plan remains.

Everything needs to be carried out during the coming night; and if we go on waiting around, it won't be possible or feasible any longer. Come on, Socrates, do all you can to take my advice, and do exactly what I say.

SOCRATES. My dear Crito, your zeal will be invaluable if b it should have right on its side; but otherwise, the greater it is, the harder it makes matters. We must therefore consider whether or not the course you urge should be followed—because it is in my nature, not just now for the first time but always, to follow nothing within me 5 but the principle* which appears to me, upon reflection, to be best.

I cannot now reject the very principles that I previously adopted, just because this fate has overtaken me; rather, they appear to me much the same as ever, and I respect and honour the same ones that I did before. If c we cannot find better ones to maintain in the present situation, you can be sure that I won't agree with you— not even if the power of the populace threatens us, like children, with more bogeymen* than it does now, by 5 visiting us with imprisonment, execution, or confiscation of property.

What, then, is the most reasonable way to consider the matter? Suppose we first take up the point you make about what people will think. Was it always an accept- d able principle that one should pay heed to some opinions but not to others, or was it not? Or was it acceptable before I had to die, while now it is exposed as an idle assertion made for the sake of talk, when it is really childish nonsense? For my part, Crito, I'm eager to look 5 into this together with you, to see whether the principle is to be viewed any differently, or in the same way, now that I'm in this position, and whether we should disregard or follow it.

As I recall, the following principle always used to be affirmed by people who thought they were talking sense: the principle, as I was just saying, that one should have a high regard for some opinions held by human beings, e but not for others. Come now, Crito: don't you think

that was a good principle? I ask because you are not, in
47a all foreseeable likelihood, going to die tomorrow, and
my present trouble shouldn't impair your judgement.
Consider, then: don't you think it a good principle, that
one shouldn't respect all human opinions, but only some
and not others; or, again, that one shouldn't respect everyone's opinions, but those of some people, and not those
5 of others? What do you say? Isn't that a good principle?

CRITO. It is.

SOCRATES. And one should respect the good ones, but not
the bad ones?

CRITO. Yes.

SOCRATES. And good ones are those of people with understanding, whereas bad ones are those of people without
10 it?

CRITO. Of course.

SOCRATES. Now then, once again, how were such points
b established?* When a man is in training, and concen-
trating upon that, does he pay heed to the praise or cen-
sure or opinion of each and every man, or only to those
of the individual who happens to be his doctor or trainer?

CRITO. Only to that individual's.

5 SOCRATES. Then he should fear the censures, and welcome the praises of that individual, but not those of
most people.*

CRITO. Obviously.

SOCRATES. So he must base his actions and exercises, his
eating and drinking, upon the opinion of the individual,
10 the expert supervisor, rather than upon everyone else's.

CRITO. True.

c SOCRATES. Very well. If he disobeys that individual and
disregards his opinion and his praises, but respects those
of most people, who are ignorant, he'll suffer harm,
won't he?

CRITO. Of course.

5 SOCRATES. And what is that harm? What does it affect?
What element within the disobedient man?

CRITO. Obviously, it affects his body, because that's what
it spoils.

SOCRATES. A good answer. And in other fields too, Crito—
we needn't go through them all, but they surely include
matters of just and unjust, honourable and dishonourable,   10
good and bad, the subjects of our present deliberation—
is it the opinion of most people that we should follow and   d
fear, or is it that of the individual authority—assuming
that some expert exists* who should be respected and
feared above all others? If we don't follow that person,
won't we corrupt and impair the element which (as we
agreed) is made better by what is just, but is spoilt by   5
what is unjust?* Or is there nothing in all that?

CRITO. I accept it myself, Socrates.

SOCRATES. Well now, if we spoil the part of us that is
improved by what is healthy but corrupted by what is
unhealthy, because it is not expert opinion that we are   10
following, are our lives worth living once it has been   e
corrupted? The part in question is, of course, the body,
isn't it?

CRITO. Yes.

SOCRATES. And are our lives worth living with a poor or
corrupted body?   5

CRITO. Definitely not.

SOCRATES. Well then, are they worth living if the element
which is impaired by what is unjust and benefited by
what is just has been corrupted? Or do we consider the
element to which justice or injustice belongs, whichever 48a
part of us it is, to be of less value than the body?

CRITO. By no means.

SOCRATES. On the contrary, it is more precious?

CRITO. Far more.

SOCRATES. Then, my good friend, we shouldn't care all   5
that much about what the populace will say of us, but
about what the expert on matters of justice and injustice will say, the individual authority, or Truth.* In the
first place, then, your proposal that we should care about
popular opinion regarding just, honourable, or good   10
actions, and their opposites, is mistaken.

'Even so,' someone might say, 'the populace has the
power to put us to death.'

b CRITO. *That*'s certainly clear enough; one might say that, Socrates.

SOCRATES. You're right. But the principle we've rehearsed, my dear friend, still remains as true as it was before—for me at any rate. And now consider this further one, to see whether or not it still holds good for us. We should attach the highest value, shouldn't we, not to

5 living, but to living well?

CRITO. Why yes, that still holds.

SOCRATES. And living well is the same as living honourably or justly?* Does that still hold or not?

CRITO. Yes, it does.

10 SOCRATES. Then in the light of those admissions, we must ask the following question: is it just, or is it not, for me

c to try to get out of here, when Athenian authorities are unwilling to release me? Then, if it does seem just, let us attempt it; but if it doesn't, let us abandon the idea.

As for the questions you raise about expenses and reputation and bringing up children, I suspect they are

5 the concerns of those who cheerfully put people to death, and would bring them back to life if they could, without any intelligence, namely, the populace. For us, however, because our principle so demands, there is no other question to ask except the one we just raised: shall we

d be acting justly—we who are rescued as well as the rescuers themselves—if we pay money and do favours to those who would get me out of here? Or shall we in truth be acting unjustly if we do all those things? And if it is clear that we shall be acting unjustly in taking that course, then the question whether we shall have to die through standing firm and holding our peace, or

5 suffer in any other way, ought not to weigh with us in comparison with acting unjustly.

CRITO. I think that's finely *said*, Socrates; but do please consider what we should *do*.

SOCRATES. Let's examine that question together, dear

e friend; and if you have objections to anything I say, please raise them, and I'll listen to you—otherwise, good fellow, it's time to stop telling me, again and again, that

I should leave here against the will of Athens. You see, I set great store upon persuading you as to my course of action, and not acting against your will. Come now, just consider whether you find the starting-point of our   5 inquiry acceptable, and try to answer my questions 49a according to your real beliefs.

CRITO. All right, I'll try.

SOCRATES. Do we maintain that people should on no account whatever do injustice willingly? Or may it be done in some circumstances but not in others? Is acting   5 unjustly in no way good or honourable, as we frequently agreed in the past? Or have all those former agreements been jettisoned during these last few days? Can it be, Crito, that men of our age have long failed to notice, as we earnestly conversed with each other, that we our-   10 selves were no better than children? Or is what we then   b used to say true above all else? Whether most people say so or not, and whether we must be treated more harshly or more leniently than at present, isn't it a fact, all the same, that acting unjustly is utterly bad and shameful for the agent? Yes or no?   5

CRITO. Yes.

SOCRATES. So one must not act unjustly at all.

CRITO. Absolutely not.

SOCRATES. Then, even if one is unjustly treated, one should not return injustice,* as most people believe—given that one should not act unjustly at all.   10

CRITO. Apparently not.   c

SOCRATES. Well now, Crito, should one ever ill-treat anybody or not?

CRITO. Surely not, Socrates.

SOCRATES. And again, when one suffers ill-treatment, is it just to return it, as most people maintain, or isn't it?   5

CRITO. It is not just at all.

SOCRATES. Because there's no difference, I take it, between ill-treating people and treating them unjustly.

CRITO. Correct.

SOCRATES. Then one shouldn't return injustice or ill-   10 treatment to any human being, no matter how one may

d   be treated by that person. And in making those admis-
       sions, Crito, watch out that you're not agreeing to any-
       thing contrary to your real beliefs.* I say that, because
       I realize that the belief is held by few people, and
       always will be. Those who hold it share no common
       counsel with those who don't; but each group is bound
       to regard the other with contempt when they observe
5   one another's decisions. You too, therefore, should con-
       sider very carefully whether you share that belief with
       me, and whether we may begin our deliberations from
       the following premiss: neither doing nor returning in-
       justice is ever right, nor should one who is ill-treated
       defend himself by retaliation. Do you agree? Or do you
e   dissent and not share my belief in that premiss? I've
       long been of that opinion myself, and I still am now;
       but if you've formed any different view, say so, and
       explain it. If you stand by our former view, however,
       then listen to my next point.

       CRITO. Well, I do stand by it and share that view, so go
       ahead.

5   SOCRATES. All right, I'll make my next point—or rather,
       ask a question. Should the things one agrees with some-
       one else be done, provided they are just,* or should one
       cheat?

       CRITO. They should be done.

       SOCRATES. Then consider what follows. If we leave this
50a   place without having persuaded our city, are we or are
       we not ill-treating certain people, indeed people whom
       we ought least of all to be ill-treating? And would we
       be abiding by the things we agreed,* those things being
       just, or not?

       CRITO. I can't answer your question, Socrates, because
5   I don't understand it.

       SOCRATES. Well, look at it this way. Suppose we were
       on the point of running away from here, or whatever
       else one should call it.* Then the Laws, or the State of
       Athens, might come and confront us, and they might
       speak as follows:
            'Please tell us, Socrates, what do you have in mind?

With this action you are attempting, do you intend any- **b**
thing short of destroying us,* the Laws and the city as
a whole, to the best of your ability? Do you think that
a city can still exist without being overturned, if the
legal judgments rendered within it possess no force, but
are nullified or invalidated by individuals?' **5**

What shall we say, Crito, in answer to that and other
such questions? Because somebody, particularly a legal
advocate,* might say a great deal on behalf of the law
that is being invalidated here, the one requiring that
judgments, once rendered, shall have authority.* Shall
we tell them: 'Yes, that is our intention, because the city **c**
was treating us unjustly, by not judging our case correctly'? Is that to be our answer, or what?

CRITO. Indeed it is, Socrates.

SOCRATES. And what if the Laws say: 'And was that also **5**
part of the agreement between you and us, Socrates? Or
did you agree to abide by whatever judgments the city
rendered?'

Then, if we were surprised by their words, perhaps
they might say: 'Don't be surprised at what we are saying, Socrates, but answer us, seeing that you like to use
question-and-answer.* What complaint, pray, do you **10**
have against the city and ourselves, that you should now **d**
attempt to destroy us? In the first place, was it not we
who gave you birth? Did your father not marry your
mother and beget you under our auspices? So will you
inform those of us here who regulate marriages whether
you have any criticism of them as poorly framed?'

'No, I have none,' I should say. **5**

'Well then, what of the laws dealing with children's
upbringing and education, under which you were educated yourself? Did those of us Laws who are in charge
of that area not give proper direction, when they required your father to educate you in the arts and phys- **e**
ical training?'*

'They did,' I should say.

'Very good. In view of your birth, upbringing, and
education, can you deny, first, that you belong to us as

our offspring and slave, as your forebears also did? And
if so, do you imagine that you are on equal terms with
us in regard to what is just, and that whatever treatment we may accord to you, it is just for you to do
the same thing back to us? You weren't on equal terms
with your father, or your master (assuming you had
one), making it just for you to return the treatment
you received—answering back when you were scolded,
or striking back when you were struck, or doing many
other things of the same sort. Will you then have licence
against your fatherland and its Laws, if we try to destroy you, in the belief that that is just? Will you try to
destroy us in return, to the best of your ability? And
will you claim that in doing so you are acting justly,
you who are genuinely exercised about goodness? Or
are you, in your wisdom, unaware that, in comparison
with your mother and father and all your other forebears, your fatherland is more precious and venerable,
more sacred and held in higher esteem among gods, as
well as among human beings who have any sense; and
that you should revere your fatherland, deferring to it
and appeasing it when it is angry,* more than your own
father? You must either persuade it, or else do whatever
it commands;* and if it ordains that you must submit to
certain treatment, then you must hold your peace and
submit to it: whether that means being beaten or put in
bonds, or whether it leads you into war to be wounded
or killed,* you must act accordingly, and that is what
is just; you must neither give way nor retreat, nor leave
your position;* rather, in warfare, in court, and everywhere else, you must do whatever your city or fatherland commands, or else persuade it as to what is truly
just;* and if it is sinful to use violence against your
mother or father, it is far more so to use it against your
fatherland.'*

What shall we say to that, Crito? That the Laws are
right or not?

CRITO. I think they are.

SOCRATES. 'Consider then, Socrates,' the Laws might go

on, 'whether the following is also true: in your present
undertaking you are not proposing to treat us justly.
We gave you birth, upbringing, and education, and a
share in all the benefits we could provide for you along   d
with all your fellow citizens. Nevertheless, we proclaim,
by the formal granting of permission, that any Athenian
who wishes, once he has been admitted to adult status,*
and has observed the conduct of city business and ourselves, the Laws, may—if he is dissatisfied with us—go
wherever he pleases* and take his property. Not one of   5
us Laws hinders or forbids that: whether any of you
wishes to emigrate to a colony, or to go and live as an
alien elsewhere, he may go wherever he pleases and   e
keep his property, if we and the city fail to satisfy him.

'We do say, however, that if any of you remains here
after he has observed the system by which we dispense
justice and otherwise manage our city, then he has agreed
with us by his conduct to obey whatever orders we give   5
him. And thus we claim that anyone who fails to obey
is guilty on three counts: he disobeys us as his parents;
he disobeys those who nurtured him; and after agreeing
to obey us he neither obeys nor persuades us if we are
doing anything amiss, even though we offer him a choice,
and do not harshly insist that he must do whatever we   52a
command. Instead, we give him two options: he must
either persuade us or else do as we say; yet he does
neither. Those are the charges, Socrates, to which we
say you too will be liable if you carry out your intention; and among Athenians, you will be not the least   5
liable, but one of the most.'

And if I were to say, 'How so?' perhaps they could
fairly reproach me, observing that I am actually among
those Athenians who have made that agreement with
them most emphatically.

'Socrates,' they would say, 'we have every indication   b
that you were content with us, as well as with our city,
because you would never have stayed home here, more
than is normal for all other Athenians,* unless you
were abnormally content. You never left our city for a   5

festival—except once to go to the Isthmus*—nor did you go elsewhere for other purposes, apart from military service. You never travelled abroad, as other people do; nor were you eager for acquaintance with a different city or different laws: we and our city sufficed for you. Thus, you emphatically opted for us, and agreed to be a citizen on our terms. In particular, you fathered children in our city, which would suggest that you were content with it.

c

'Moreover, during your actual trial it was open to you, had you wished, to propose exile as your penalty; thus, what you are now attempting to do without the city's consent, you could then have done with it. On that occasion, you kept priding yourself that it would not trouble you if you had to die: you would choose death ahead of exile, so you said.* Yet now you dishonour those words, and show no regard for us, the Laws, in your effort to destroy us. You are acting as the meanest slave would act, by trying to run away* in spite of those compacts and agreements you made with us, whereby you agreed to be a citizen on our terms.

5

d

'First, then, answer us this question: are we right in claiming that you agreed, by your conduct if not verbally, that you would be a citizen on our terms? Or is that untrue?'

5

What shall we say in reply to that, Crito? Mustn't we agree?

CRITO. We must, Socrates.

SOCRATES. 'Then what does your action amount to,' they would say, 'except breaking the compacts and agreements you made with us? By your own admission, you were not coerced or tricked into making them, or forced to reach a decision in a short time: you had seventy years* in which it was open to you to leave if you were not happy with us, or if you thought those agreements unfair. Yet you preferred neither Lacedaemon nor Crete* —places you often say are well governed—nor any other Greek or foreign city: in fact, you went abroad less often than the lame and the blind or other cripples. Obviously,

e

5

53a

then, amongst Athenians you were exceptionally content with our city and with us, its Laws—because who
would care for a city apart from its laws? Won't you,   5
then, abide by your agreements now? Yes you will, if
you listen to us, Socrates; and then at least you won't
make yourself an object of derision by leaving the city.

'Just consider: if you break those agreements, and
commit any of those offences, what good will you do   10
yourself or those friends of yours? Your friends, pretty   b
obviously, will risk being exiled themselves, as well as
being disenfranchised or losing their property. As for
you, first of all, if you go to one of the nearest cities,
Thebes or Megara*—they are both well governed—you   5
will arrive as an enemy of their political systems, Socrates: all who are concerned for their own cities will
look askance at you, regarding you as a subverter of
laws.* You will also confirm your jurors in their judgment, making them think they decided your case cor-   c
rectly: any subverter of laws, presumably, might well be
thought to be a corrupter of young, unthinking people.

'Will you, then, avoid the best-governed cities and
the most respectable of men? And if so, will your life be
worth living? Or will you associate with those people,   5
and be shameless enough to converse with them? And
what will you say to them, Socrates? The things you
used to say here, that goodness and justice are most
precious to mankind, along with institutions and laws?
Don't you think that the predicament of Socrates will
cut an ugly figure? Surely you must.   d

'Or will you take leave of those spots, and go to stay
with those friends of Crito's up in Thessaly?* That, of
course, is a region of the utmost disorder and licence; so
perhaps they would enjoy hearing from you about your
comical escape from gaol, when you dressed up in some   5
outfit, wore a leather jerkin or some other runaway's
garb, and altered your appearance. Will no one observe
that you, an old man with probably only a short time
left to live, had the nerve to cling so greedily to life by e
violating the most important laws? Perhaps not, so long

as you don't trouble anyone. Otherwise, Socrates, you
will hear a great deal to your own discredit. You will
live as every person's toady and lackey; and what will
5   you be doing—apart from living it up in Thessaly, as if
you had travelled all the way to Thessaly to have din-
54a   ner? As for those principles of yours about justice and
goodness in general—tell us, where will they be then?

'Well then, is it for your children's sake that you wish
to live, in order to bring them up and give them an
education? How so? Will you bring them up and educate them by taking them off to Thessaly and making
5   foreigners of them, so that they may gain that advantage too? Or if, instead of that, they are brought up
here, will they be better brought up and educated just
because you are alive, if you are not with them? Yes,
you may say, because those friends of yours will take
care of them. Then will they take care of them if you
10   travel to Thessaly, but not take care of them if you
travel to Hades?* Surely if those professing to be your
b   friends are of any use at all, you must believe that they
will.

'No, Socrates, listen to us, your own nurturers: do
not place a higher value upon children, upon life, or
upon anything else, than upon what is just, so that
5   when you leave for Hades, this may be your whole
defence before the authorities there: to take that course
seems neither better nor more just or holy, for you or
for any of your friends here in this world. Nor will it
be better for you when you reach the next. As things
c   stand, you will leave this world (if you do) as one who
has been treated unjustly not by us Laws, but by human
beings;* whereas if you go into exile, thereby shame-
fully returning injustice for injustice and ill-treatment for
ill-treatment, breaking the agreements and compacts you
made with us, and inflicting harm upon the people you
5   should least harm—yourself, your friends, your fatherland, and ourselves—then we shall be angry with you in
your lifetime; and our brother Laws in Hades will not
receive you kindly there, knowing that you tried, to the

best of your ability, to destroy us too. Come then, do   d
not let Crito persuade you to take his advice rather than
ours.'

That, Crito, my dear comrade, is what I seem to hear
them saying, I do assure you. I am like the Corybantic
revellers* who think they are still hearing the music of
pipes: the sound of those arguments is ringing loudly   5
in my head, and makes me unable to hear the others.
As far as these present thoughts of mine go, then, you
may be sure that if you object to them, you will plead
in vain. None the less, if you think you will do any
good, speak up.

CRITO. No, Socrates, I've nothing to say.

SOCRATES. Then let it be, Crito, and let us act accord-   e
ingly, because that is the direction in which God* is
guiding us.

EXPLANATORY NOTES

EUTHYPHRO

2a *the Lyceum*: a gymnasium outside the walls of Athens, and a favourite resort of Socrates, where the philosophical discussions in Plato's dialogues are sometimes set. Cf. *Euthydemus* 271a, *Symposium* 223d, *Lysis* 203a.

the King Archon: the archons were nine officials chosen annually as Athens' chief magistrates. The 'King Archon' was one of their number chosen by lot, with special responsibility for religious ceremonial and ritual purification, and for cases involving offences against state religion. His Porch was in the Agora or market-place. Euthyphro and Socrates both have preliminary business there in connection with their lawsuits.

lawsuit . . . indictment: the general term 'lawsuit' (*dikē*) included private actions brought to redress wrong done to the litigant, whereas an 'indictment' (*graphē*) was prosecution for an injury to the state. Both types of action were initiated by private citizens.

2b *the Pitthean deme*: a deme was one of the divisions, originally territorial, upon which the registration of Athenian voters was based.

3a *a good start at damaging the city*: literally, 'damaging the city from its hearth'. A sacred flame was kept burning at a hearth in the city's seat of government. In suggesting that an attack on Socrates is a blow at the heart of the state, Euthyphro dissociates himself from the prosecution.

3b *your spiritual sign*: for this source of guidance, see *Defence of Socrates* 31c–d, 40a–b. Euthyphro's assumption that it explained Socrates' indictment is supported by *Defence* 31d. The 'sign' was evidently well known, and may have helped to give credence to the charges of religious innovation, although these were clearly brought on other grounds as well. See note on *Defence* 31d and Introduction, pp. xxii–xxiii.

3c *the Assembly*: the sovereign body of Athenian democracy. All adult male citizens were eligible to attend its meetings and to vote.

3d *my benevolence*: Socrates represents his philosophical activities as altruistic. Cf. *Defence* 31b, where he takes this fact to indicate

81

that they are enjoined by God. See Introduction, p. xiv, and note on 31b.

3e *with intelligence*: literally, 'according to intelligence'. For 'intelligence' as a source of moral guidance, see Introduction, p. xxiii.

4a *Are you chasing a bird on the wing?*: the verb translated 'chase' can also mean 'prosecute'. The phrase was proverbial. Socrates imagines that Euthyphro's action as prosecutor is, as we would say, 'a wild goose chase'.

4c *Naxos*: a large island in the Cyclades, the group of Aegean islands lying to the south-east of Attica.

the religious authority: this official was an interpreter of religious law, who gave advice upon procedures for purification in homicide cases.

5d *the pious and the impious ... the holy ... the unholy*: Greek phrases of the form 'the X' can mean either the property X or that which possesses it. When Socrates asks about 'the pious' or 'the holy', he wishes to understand more clearly what it means to ascribe that property to an action or a person, and to discover a criterion for doing so. No distinction seems intended between 'pious' and 'holy'. Both adjectives (and their negations) occur frequently with the definite article, and have been so translated. 'Holiness' and 'piety' have been used only in the few places where Plato uses abstract nouns. See also note on 6d.

in itself similar to itself: unholiness, considered in and of itself, is always alike wherever it occurs. Like holiness, it is a single nature common to all items that possess it.

possessed of a single character: the word translated 'character' (*idea*) is the ancestor of the English 'idea'. Socrates is not, however, seeking an 'idea' in the sense of a subjective or mind-dependent entity. He is seeking an objective property, common to all of the many holy (or unholy) items, in virtue of which they are so called. At 6d the word *eidos* is used for that property, and has been translated 'form'. The passage is sometimes thought to anticipate the doctrine known to modern philosophers (though not to Plato himself) as the 'theory of forms'. The 'theory', a central theme in many Platonic dialogues, originated, in part, from Socrates' searches for definitions of ethical terms, of which the *Euthyphro* provides an example. However, most scholars would now deny that the Platonic theory, as elaborated in such dialogues as the *Phaedo*, *Symposium*, and *Republic*, was held by the historical Socrates. See also note on 6d.

6a *put his father in bonds*: the theology of this passage is condemned in the *Republic* (376c–383c, esp. 378a–e). Already, a century before Plato, the philosopher-poet Xenophanes had criticized the immoral behaviour of the gods in the poetry of Homer and Hesiod. See his fragments 11–12, discussed by J. H. Lesher, *Xenophanes of Colophon* (Toronto, 1992), 82–5. See also Index of Names, s.v. Cronus, and Introduction, p. xi.

6b *the gods actually make war upon one another*: strife amongst the gods abounds in Homer's *Iliad* and *Odyssey*, and is a mainspring for the plots of both epics. It is also rampant in Hesiod's *Theogony*.

6c *the Acropolis . . . the great Panathenaean festival*: the Acropolis was the large rocky eminence which dominates Athens. It was the site of various temples, including the renowned Parthenon, sacred to the city's patron goddess Athena. A festival called 'Panathenaea' was held annually to celebrate her birthday. Every four years the celebration took a more elaborate form, and was called the 'great' Panathenaea. The ceremonial robe mentioned here was embroidered for a statue of Athena. It depicted a savage battle between gods and giants, to which Plato alludes at *Republic* 378c–d. The Parthenon contained a famous frieze representing the Panathenaean procession.

6d *the form itself*: the role of Platonic 'forms' (for which see note on 5d) in settling ethical disputes is explained here. The form is said to function as a 'model' or 'exemplar' (*paradeigma*), enabling particular items to be described as possessing or lacking a given property, according as they conform, or fail to conform, to the model. Thus one motivation for philosophical inquiry is the hope of settling disagreements by finding a *standard* to which appeal can be made in disputed cases.

7a *loved-by-the-gods . . . hated-by-the-gods*: these hyphenated phrases translate compound adjectives meaning 'what is loved by the gods' and 'what is hated by the gods' respectively. They have been hyphenated to mark the fact that 'the holy' and 'the unholy' are here defined in terms of single Greek words, 'god-beloved' (*theophiles*) and 'god-hated' (*theomises*).

7c *would we resort to counting . . . them?*: this passage contains (*a*) the important notion of a 'decision procedure' for settling disputed cases; and (*b*) a contrast between ethical predicates, for which no such procedure exists, and predicates of number and size, for which counting, weighing, and measuring are available. Here as elsewhere in Plato the mathematical sciences provide a model for philosophy to emulate in the sphere of value judgements. For the idea of measurement in settling ethical disputes, cf. especially *Protagoras* 356a–357b.

7d *just and unjust*: the Greek adjectives (*dikaios* and *adikos*) can be used of both actions and persons, whereas the English 'right' and 'wrong' belong, in their moral sense, only to actions. The adjectives have therefore usually been translated 'just' and 'unjust', but their scope is often much wider, covering honesty, rectitude, or morality in general. The cognate verb *adikein* has been translated 'to act unjustly', 'to do injustice', or (when transitive) 'to treat unjustly'.

8a *what selfsame thing*: Socrates harks back to his earlier quest for an account of 'the holy' as 'the same as itself in every action' (5d). If 'the holy' is always 'the same as itself', it cannot be identified with a character that is common to both holy and unholy things. Socrates has just shown that certain things which are 'loved-by-the-gods' are also 'hated-by-the-gods'. It follows that 'loved-by-the-gods' cannot be the definition of 'the holy'.

8b *agreeable to Zeus but odious to Cronus and Uranus*: Socrates recalls the example that Euthyphro had used to justify his prosecution of his father. The story of Hephaestus and Hera also illustrates the mistreatment of parent by offspring. For the story, see Index of Names, s.v. Hephaestus. See also note on 6a, and Introduction, p. xi.

8e *no one ... should go unpunished who has acted unjustly*: this principle will be important for the argument of the *Crito*. See Introduction, pp. xxix–xxxi. Neither Socrates nor Euthyphro allows any scope for extenuating circumstances.

10a *is the holy loved by the gods because it is holy? Or is it holy because it is loved?*: this conundrum is the most powerful philosophical question raised by the dialogue. See Introduction, pp. xi–xiii. Unfortunately, Socrates' 'clarification' of it leads into one of the most elusive arguments in all of Plato's writings. Its interpretation and validity have been much debated.

how they differ: Socrates distinguishes active from passive participles of the verbs 'carry', 'lead', and 'see', and suggests a parallel distinction for 'love'. The distinction is between the agent which bestows a certain treatment on something and the recipient of that treatment. We would naturally speak of the difference between 'subject' and 'object', but Plato lacks a developed grammatical terminology.

10b *because someone is carrying it*: the translation, though not faithful to Plato's grammar, is in keeping with the distinction drawn above between the agent and the recipient of a given treatment (see previous note), and preserves the general sense of the argument. The Greek verbs in the present sentence (and their counterparts in the following argument) are all passive in form. English verbs, however, lack distinct passive-voice forms to mark the contrast Socrates is drawing. The translation therefore uses active forms, 'someone is carrying it' (and corresponding phrases for the other examples), to bring out the essential contrast between (*a*) the *state* into which a thing is brought and (*b*) the *treatment* by an agent which gets it into that state. Compare the use of 'dressed' in (*a*) 'the bride was dressed in white', and (*b*) 'the bride was dressed by her mother'.

10c *what I mean is this*: Socrates now generalizes from his examples. The 'state' of a subject depends upon its having the relevant 'treatment' bestowed upon it. It is assumed that if something is 'X because it is Y', then it cannot also be 'Y because it is X'. The state depends upon the treatment, and not vice versa. The nature of this dependence remains unclear, however, since the meaning of 'because' is left unexplained, and is capable of various interpretations.

'being loved' is a case of . . . agent: Socrates here secures a premiss that might be doubted—namely, that 'being loved' is parallel to the previous examples of 'being carried', 'being led', and 'being seen'. In one respect, at least, it seems more akin to 'being seen' than to 'being carried' or 'being led': an object cannot be carried or led without alteration of its position, whereas it can be loved or seen without being altered in any way at all.

10d *No, that is the reason*: with this response Euthyphro grants a crucial point, which is significant for the ethical position of the whole dialogue. For its implications, see Introduction, pp. xi–xii.

By contrast, what is loved-by-the-gods: the translation at 10d10 depends on an emended text (see textual note). The emendation, though not essential, greatly helps to clarify the argument, by making 'what is loved-by-the-gods' the subject of the sentence instead of 'the holy', thereby highlighting the way in which Socrates is contrasting the two notions.

10e *But if what is loved-by-the-gods and the holy were the same thing...*: the argument depends upon taking Euthyphro's definition of 'holy' as 'loved-by-the-gods' to allow those terms to be *interchanged* in the statements that follow.

It is assumed that if Euthyphro's definition of 'holy' as 'loved-by-the-gods' were correct, then either term could be substituted for the other without altering the truth of the statements in which they occur. Socrates proceeds to show, however, that if the terms are interchanged in two statements that Euthyphro has already granted, they generate a further pair of statements inconsistent with those two.

Thus, from

(A1) the holy is loved because it is holy,
by substituting 'loved-by-the-gods' for 'holy',

we can derive:

(A2) what is loved-by-the-gods is loved because it is loved-by-the-gods.

And from

(B1) what is loved-by-the-gods is loved-by-the-gods because the gods love it,

by substituting 'holy' for 'loved-by-the-gods', we can derive:

(B2) the holy is holy because the gods love it.

But A2 is inconsistent with B1, and B2 with A1. Yet Euthyphro has committed himself to A1 and B1 at 10d. Therefore he must admit that the definition which has enabled A2 and B2 to be derived from A1 and B1 is incorrect.

The unstated principle underlying this elegant argument is that two terms with the same meaning can be interchanged in any statement without altering its truth. For other examples in Plato, compare *Protagoras* 355b–e and *Phaedo* 93d. The legitimacy of its use in the present argument is highly questionable.

11a *one of them is lovable because they love it, whereas the other they love for the reason that it is lovable*: 'one of them' refers to 'the god-beloved', and 'the other' to 'the holy'. It is unclear exactly what the expression 'lovable' (literally, 'such as to be loved') signifies, but Socrates appears to be reiterating that what is loved-by-the-gods is in that 'state' merely by virtue of the gods' loving it; whereas what is holy is loved by the gods because it has a property affording them a *ground* for loving it—namely, the property of being holy. If that is the meaning, Plato is making the important point that value is not conferred upon a thing merely by virtue of someone's (even God's) approving it. One's approval of something cannot be the *reason* for which one approves it. Rather, any rational approver can approve of a thing only for some quality that it possesses independently of its being approved. For the wider implication of this point, see Introduction, p. xii.

you'd prefer not to explain its essence to me, but would rather tell me one of its properties: the words rendered 'essence' (*ousia*) and 'property' (*pathos*) are used to distinguish between essential and accidental features of an item. 'Being approved by the gods' is not, as we would say, an essential feature of holy actions, but one which they just happen to possess.

11b *we won't disagree about that*: Socrates does not wish to argue about whether all holy actions *are*, in fact, approved by the gods. He simply sets the point aside as irrelevant. For even if it be granted that all holy actions are approved by the gods, divine approval is not what *constitutes* their holiness. The point is sometimes expressed by saying that even if 'holy' and 'loved-by-the-gods' have the same extension (i.e. even if all holy things are also loved-by-the-gods, and conversely), the two terms do not have the same meaning.

My ancestor Daedalus: because Socrates refers to Daedalus (for whom see Index of Names) as his 'ancestor', this text has been thought to confirm the later tradition that Socrates' father was a stonemason, and that Socrates practised that trade himself. The statues of Daedalus, however, appear to have been made of wood. There is no contemporary evidence that Socrates ever practised statuary. At *Defence* 22d he disclaims knowledge of any craft at all.

11c *my works of art in conversation run away*: the moving statues of Daedalus reappear in the *Meno* (97d–e), to represent opinions which are unstable because they lack rational foundation. They illustrate the important Platonic distinction between 'true opinion' and 'knowledge'. In the present passage and at 15b, they represent the successive definitions of holiness, all of which have proved unstable, thus suggesting that neither Socrates nor Euthyphro has knowledge.

11e *you are being feeble*: the Greek verb signifies a bloated condition, characteristic of those who live in luxury. Socrates pretends that Euthyphro's poor appetite for the inquiry is due to the excessive wealth of wisdom in which he is rolling.

12a *Is part of it holy, and part of it something else?*: the word 'part' is used to mark off holy actions as a sub-class of the wider class of just ones. Thus, Socrates will suggest that all holy actions are just, but not all just actions are holy. This is unlikely to have been either his or Plato's own view. See Introduction, p. xiii.

12b *With Zeus, who wrought it . . . there is also shame*: the text and exact sense of the quotation are uncertain. It is attributed in later tradition to Stasinus of Cyprus, an early epic poet.

12c *doesn't anyone who is ashamed . . . a reputation for wickedness*: it is notable that shame is explained as a kind of fear. Fear of unholy conduct is what Euthyphro ought to feel but does not (4e). See note on 15d and Introduction, p. xv.

12d *not scalene . . . but isosceles*: Greek mathematicians thought of numbers by analogy with geometrical figures. An isosceles triangle has two equal sides, whereas a scalene triangle has none. Hence, an even number is 'isosceles', because it can be divided into two equal parts which are both whole numbers, whereas an odd number is 'scalene', because it cannot be so divided.

14c *you were on the very brink of the answer*: for the implication of this, see Introduction, pp. xiii–xiv.

the questioner must follow wherever the person questioned may lead him: this translation follows the revised OCT. Burnet's text gives the sense 'a lover must follow wherever his beloved may lead him'. With that text, either Socrates is treating Euthyphro as his 'spoilt darling' who must be humoured (cf. 11e–12a, *Meno* 76b); or else Socrates is a 'lover' of the argument, which he is bound to follow wherever it may lead him. Neither alternative seems very natural in the context. With the revised OCT, the point is simply that since Euthyphro has not picked up the clue that might have led him to a correct solution, Socrates is obliged to adapt his questioning to the poor response he has actually received.

14e *Trading, yes, if that's what you prefer to call it*: for the implication of Euthyphro's grudging assent, see Introduction, p. xiv.

15b *So the holy is gratifying, but not beneficial or loved by the gods?*: Socrates is not justified in inferring that the holy is not loved by the gods. Since esteem and honour are gratifying to them, there remains good reason for Euthyphro to hold that they love holy actions. Hence his emphatic retort, that the holy is 'the most loved of all things', seems in order.

Then, once again . . . what is loved by the gods: Socrates inter-prets Euthyphro's assertion that the holy is 'most loved of all things' by the gods, as if 'being most loved by the gods' defined the holy. But 'the holy is the most loved of all things by the gods' no more defines the holy than 'the string quartet is the most loved of all musical forms by Haydn' defines the string quartet. Only by putting an unintended spin on Euthyphro's words can Socrates claim that he has reverted to an earlier definition. See note on 15c.

will you blame me as the Daedalus: see note on 11c.

15c *that makes it identical with loved-by-the-gods, doesn't it?*: the phrase 'what the gods love' is equated with a single compound adjective, 'loved-by-the-gods'. See note on 7a. Once again, 'the holy is loved by the gods' is treated as if it meant 'the holy is (identical with) that which is loved-by-the-gods'. Euthyphro's assertion of an important fact *about* the holy is misinterpreted as a statement of identity. This enables Socrates to make out that it harks back to the definition of the holy rejected at 11a–b. See note on 15b.

15d *like Proteus*: by comparing his interlocutor with Proteus (for whom see Index of Names), Socrates insinuates that he lacks any fixed identity because he lacks any stable position on the matters under discussion. For the comparison with Proteus cf. *Ion* 541e, *Euthydemus* 288b–c.

fear of the gods . . . embarrassed in front of human beings: this recalls the use of fear and shame as examples at 12b–c, where shame was explained as a kind of fear. So here, what Euthyphro feared to do before the gods he would be ashamed to do in front of human beings. See Introduction, p. xv.

16a *a free-thinker or innovator . . . I would live better for what remains of my life*: Socrates alludes to the terms of Meletus' indictment (3b), and perhaps also to the very short time that now remains for him to live.

DEFENCE OF SOCRATES

17a *I don't know*: it is striking that the *Defence of Socrates* begins, as it ends, with a disavowal of knowledge. See note on 42a.

fellow Athenians: Socrates addresses his judges in this way, instead of the more usual 'gentlemen of the jury', partly be-cause he will later refuse to recognize those who voted against him as 'jurors' at all. See note on 40a. The mode of address may also appeal, as do portions of his speech (29d–e, 34e–35b), to the jurors' pride as Athenian citizens.

18b *a 'wise man'*: *sophos* has generally been rendered 'wise', and *sophia* 'wisdom'. A different word (*phronēsis*), often given as 'wisdom', has been translated 'understanding'. Although Plato draws no clear-cut distinction between these terms, they tend to have different resonances in his usage. In particular, (i) *sophia*, unlike *phronēsis*, can cover expertise in specific fields of knowledge, as well as 'wisdom' in general; and (ii) irony can often be heard in its use. In some contexts, therefore, 'expert', 'learned', 'clever', or 'smart' will capture the flavour of *sophos* better than 'wise'.

18c *turns the weaker argument into the stronger*: Socrates' reputation for skill in argument enabled Aristophanes to caricature him as an instructor in logical trickery. Cf. *Clouds* 112–15. The play also features a debate between Right and Wrong, in which the latter prevails (889–1104). Chicanery in argument is brilliantly satirized, and contrasted with the methods of Socrates, in Plato's *Euthydemus*. 'Turning the weaker argument into the stronger' was evidently regarded as a trade mark of the late fifth-century sophistic movement. Training in it is reported by Aristotle to have been offered by the famous sophist Protagoras, and to have been unpopular (*Rhetoric* 1402a23–6). For the sophists, see also note on 20a, and Introduction, pp. xviii–xix.

fail to acknowledge the gods: 'failing to acknowledge the gods' was one of the formal charges against Socrates, quoted at 24b–c. It is ambiguous, since the verb translated 'acknowledge' could mean either 'worship' or 'believe', or some combination of the two. Belief seems more likely to be in point here, since an interest in scientific explanation was associated, in Socrates' time as in ours, with atheism. Cf. especially *Clouds* 358–427. When Socrates responds to the charge, it is taken to mean not that he fails to worship the gods, but that he denies their existence (26c).

18d *one who happens to be a comic playwright*: the reference is to Aristophanes, for whom see 19c, note on 18c, Index of Names, and Introduction, pp. viii, xviii–xix.

19a *in so short a time*: speeches in Athenian lawcourts were timed. Socrates reflects on the constraint this places on lawyers, and contrasts their life with the leisure of philosophers, at *Theaetetus* 172d–e. Because a jury has limited time in which to learn, and no first-hand experience of the events about which they must judge, their verdicts can at best express 'true belief' as distinct from 'knowledge' (cf. *Theaetetus* 201a–c).

I should like to succeed in my defence: this is in direct conflict with the testimony of Xenophon, that Socrates had no serious interest in acquittal. See note on 41d, and Introduction, pp. xvi–xvii.

I have to obey the law: this is one of several places in the *Defence* in which Socrates registers his respect for the law. For others, see Introduction, p. xxxii.

19c *swings around, claims to be walking on air*: this describes Socrates' first appearance in the *Clouds* (223–5), where he is swung around in a basket in the air, and says he is walking on air and thinking about the sun.

19d *those subjects are not my concern at all*: in the *Phaedo* (96a–b) Socrates recounts his early intellectual development, and professes to have been interested, as a young man, in questions about the physical world. That story need not be taken to contradict his present statement, which does not mean that he had no interest in scientific matters, but only that they were not the subject of his own distinctive inquiries.

20a *sophists*: professional educators who offered instruction in many subjects. Socrates' present reference to eminent sophists is tinged with irony. Plato's *Protagoras* is devoted to contrasting their approach to education with that of Socrates. See also Index of Names, s.vv. Evenus, Gorgias, Hippias, Prodicus, Introduction, p. xix, and notes on 18c, 33a.

20b *he charges 5 minas*: a mina equalled 100 silver drachmas. At the end of the fifth century a drachma was roughly equivalent to one day's pay for a man employed in public works. Evenus' fees were therefore not as 'modest' as Socrates pretends. They were ten times the amount charged by Prodicus for his 50-drachma course on names. Socrates compares that with a course for only 1 drachma, which was all he could afford himself (*Cratylus* 384b). We cannot seriously assess Evenus' fees without knowing more of the nature and duration of his course. In any case, Socrates is slyly insinuating that tuition which genuinely provided what Evenus claimed to impart would have been a bargain at *any* price.

20e *the people I just mentioned*: the sophists mentioned at 19e.

the god at Delphi: for Delphi, see Introduction, p. xix. The god Apollo, though nowhere named in the *Defence*, is the deity whose servant Socrates claims to be (*Phaedo* 85b). In what follows, however, when he speaks of 'the god', it is not always clear whether he means Apollo, or a personal God distinct from any deity of traditional Greek religion. Direct reference to Apollo is clearly intended at 21b, 21e, 22a, 23a–c. Later, however (28e, 30a, 30e, 31a, 35d, 41d–42a), the reference is less definite, and 'God' or 'my god' has been used in the translation. See also notes on 42a and *Crito* 54e.

21a *your recent exile and restoration*: politicians of the democratic party had fled from Athens during the regime of the Thirty Tyrants. They returned under an amnesty in 403 when the Thirty were overthrown. See also Index of Names, s.v. Chaerephon.

the Pythia responded: see Introduction, p. xix. The verb used here for 'response' of the priestess seems to have been used originally for the picking up of a bean, i.e. drawing a lot, but nothing is known of the procedure in Chaerephon's case.

21b *What can his riddle mean?*: Heraclitus (early fifth-century philosopher) recognized the riddling character of the Delphic oracle, when he declared: 'the lord whose oracle is in Delphi neither indicates clearly nor conceals, but gives a sign' (fragment 93, trans. T. M. Robinson, *Heraclitus* (Toronto, 1987), 57, 143–4). Socrates' determination to probe the god's 'riddle' is in keeping with this tradition. For riddles see also note on 27a.

out of the question: a solemn expression, suggesting a religious prohibition, a violation of the divine order of things, and therefore unthinkable. Cf. 30d and *Phaedo* 61c–d. The belief that lying or deceit is 'out of the question' for a deity remained a basic conviction of Plato, strongly at variance with poetic tradition. Cf. *Republic* 382c–e.

22a *upon my word*: literally, 'by the dog!', a favourite Socratic oath, which may have originated as a euphemism. It occurs also at *Phaedo* 99a, and at *Gorgias* 482b, where it is linked with 'the god of the Egyptians'. See E. R. Dodds, ed., *Gorgias* (Oxford, 1959), 262–3.

the various 'labours' I kept undertaking: Socrates alludes to the labours of Heracles, twelve tasks of prodigious difficulty imposed upon a hero of legendary strength and courage.

22b *dithyrambic poets*: the dithyramb was an emotionally powerful lyric poem, performed by a chorus of singers and dancers. It was believed by Aristotle to have been the genre from which tragic drama had evolved.

I soon realized this truth about them too: Socrates speaks as if the conclusion he is about to draw regarding the poets was one he had already drawn regarding the politicians. He had not, however, ascribed divine inspiration to the latter in our text. Only in the *Meno* (99b–e) is that conclusion explicitly drawn for politicians. For a possible explanation, and its implications for the dating of the *Defence*, see De Strycker and Slings (Bibliography, item 16), 66, 282–3.

22c *seers and soothsayers*: the comparison reflects the important Platonic theme that poetry is the product of divine inspiration, not of genuine knowledge. It is typical of those who are inspired to be unable to give a rational explanation of their achievements. The theme is echoed in the *Meno* at the expense of politicians (see previous note), and is elaborated for poets in the *Ion* (533d–535a). For a related line of thought, cf. *Timaeus* 71e–72b.

23a *human wisdom is worth little or nothing*: philosophy, embodied in Socrates, is here depicted as an intermediate state between human ignorance and divine knowledge. The philosopher lies between most human beings and God, in that he is conscious of his ignorance, aspires to knowledge, but has not yet attained it. The same idea, which underlies the traditional definition of philosophy as 'love of wisdom', appears at *Symposium* 204a–c.

23b *I assist the god*: for 'service' to the gods, see *Euthyphro* 13d–14b, where the notion is differently interpreted, and Socrates' own conception of 'service to God' is not allowed to surface. See also note on 20e, and Introduction, pp. xiii–xiv.

24a *Meletus ... for the poets ... Anytus for the craftsmen ... Lycon for the orators*: it is not clear why Socrates aligns his accusers in this way. Meletus may have been the son of a poet of the same name. Anytus speaks for craftsmen as well as politicians, perhaps because he was a master-tanner, and can thus represent 'business men in government' (Burnet (Bibliography, item 9), 99). Lycon was a politician with no special reputation as an orator, though Diogenes Laertius (ii. 38) calls him a 'demagogue'. See also Index of Names, s.vv. Anytus, Lycon, Meletus.

24c *Socrates is guilty ... new spiritual beings*: Plato's version of the indictment differs from those of Xenophon (*Memorabilia* i. 1. 1) and Diogenes Laertius (ii. 40), which are probably historically more accurate. Plato reverses the order of the charges, placing 'corrupting the young' first. This perhaps reflects the greater importance attached by him to that charge, and the greater seriousness of Socrates' defence against it. See note on 26b and Introduction, p. xviii.

never cared at all: Socrates' repeated references to 'caring' in his interrogation of Meletus (cf. 24d, 25c) contain a play upon his accuser's name, whose first syllable is also the root of verbs and nouns for 'care'.

25a *the Council*: the Athenian Council was a body of 500, with fifty members from each of the ten tribes, elected annually by lot from citizens over the age of 30. In conjunction with the magistrates it carried on state business, and prepared an agenda for the Assembly (for which see note on *Euthyphro* 3c). See also note on 32b below.

25b *a single person . . . lay people spoil them*: this line of thought is of great importance for the argument of the *Crito*. See, especially, 47b–48a.

26a *I am doing so unintentionally*: Socrates' denial that he corrupts the young intentionally (cf. 37a) relies upon the principle that human beings never intentionally follow a course of action which they know or believe to be harmful to themselves. Since, in Socrates' view, all wrongdoing is harmful to the agent, it follows that all wrongdoing is unintentional, and curable by the removal of ignorance. This doctrine, one of the so-called Socratic Paradoxes, is often summarized in the slogan 'Virtue is Knowledge'. It is elaborated in the *Meno* (77b–78a) and *Protagoras* (352a–358b).

26b *I am corrupting them by teaching them that*: here the two counts of Meletus' indictment are linked, in that 'corrupting the youth' consisted in teaching them atheistic doctrines. This enables Socrates to dispose of the whole indictment by arguing that the charge of atheism was self-contradictory. That charge had stemmed partly from his enemies' total ignorance of philosophical inquiry (23d). But it still remains for him to meet the charge of 'corruption' independently of its connection with atheistic teaching. This he will do below, especially at 29d–31b and 33a–34b. For the relation between the two counts of the indictment, see also note on 24c and Introduction, p. xviii.

26d *the sun and the moon are gods*: the sun and moon, even though not the objects of an official cult at Athens, were widely believed to be divine. In the *Cratylus* (397c–d) the belief is attributed by Socrates to 'the earliest people in Greece'. Cf. *Laws* 886d–e, 887d–e. In the *Symposium* (220d) Socrates is reported to have addressed a prayer to the sun at sunrise, and he expressly calls the sun, and other heavenly bodies, 'gods' at *Republic* 508a.

do you imagine that it is Anaxagoras you are accusing?: according to one tradition, Anaxagoras (for whom see Index of Names) had been prosecuted for heresies regarding the composition of the sun and moon. The historicity and the date of Anaxagoras' trial are controversial, and the present text does not prove that it ever occurred. But if it did, Meletus betrays his ignorance by raking up an old charge that had no relevance to Socrates' beliefs or behaviour.

26e *at the bookstalls*: literally 'from the *orchēstra*'. The *orchēstra* was an area in the Agora. The young men may have heard Anaxagoras' works being read aloud there, just as Socrates says he once heard a book of Anaxagoras being read (*Phaedo* 97b). If so, the charge of a drachma will have been for hearing Anaxagoras' doctrines rather than for buying his books.

27a *a . . . riddle . . . my nice self-contradiction*: the 'riddle' which Socrates attributes to Meletus consists in the self-contradictory statement 'Socrates acknowledges gods and does not acknowledge gods'. Greek riddles often take the form of paradoxes generated by apparent self-contradiction. The challenge is to find a subject which is both X and not-X at the same time. Compare our 'when is a door not a door?' An elaborate riddle of this type, comprising no fewer than six self-contradictory descriptions, is mentioned at *Republic* 479b–c. For Greek riddles in general, see D. Gallop in *Ionian Philosophy*, ed. K. J. Boudouris (Athens, 1989), 123–35.

27b *in my usual manner*: i.e. by question-and-answer, cf. 17c–d. In the following interrogation, as at 20a–b, Socrates also shows his fondness for homespun examples and analogies.

musicians . . . musical phenomena: Socrates refers specifically to players of the *aulos*, which is commonly translated 'flute', but has no English equivalent. The instrument more closely resembled an oboe or clarinet.

27c *spiritual phenomena . . . spiritual beings*: Socrates' logic is suspect. Here he picks up the exact language of Meletus' indictment (24b–c), which had referred to 'spiritual beings' (*daimonia*) but had not used the noun translated 'phenomena' (*pragmata*) essential to the analogies in 27b. Yet, on the strength of those analogies, Meletus is now compelled to admit that Socrates accepts the existence of 'spirits' (*daimones*). For the status of 'spirits', as intermediate between the human and the divine, see *Symposium* 202d–203a, and note on 23a.

27d *children of gods*: spirits were sometimes begotten by gods through union with nymphs or mortals. In Socrates' comical analogy, horses correspond to gods, asses to their sexual partners, and mules to spirits. The Greek for 'mule' (*hēmionos*, meaning 'half-ass') is of the same form as the word for 'demi-god' (*hēmitheos*), used of Achilles and other heroes at 28c below. The verbal parallel may have suggested the analogy to Plato. The present argument is loosely paraphrased by Aristotle at *Rhetoric* 1419a5–12.

28c *the plain of Troy*: site of the legendary war between the Greeks and Trojans, which is the context of Homer's *Iliad*.

the son of Thetis: Achilles, heroic Greek warrior in the Trojan War. As the offspring of a goddess mother by a mortal father, he is referred to as a 'demigod'. The words quoted are a version of lines from *Iliad* xviii. 95–104. See also Index of Names, s.vv. Hector, Patroclus, Thetis.

28e *Potidaea, Amphipolis, or Delium*: Potidaea, in Thrace, was the scene of a campaign in 432 BC recounted in Thucydides i. 56–65. Socrates' endurance of extreme hardship there is described in Plato's *Symposium* 219e–220e. For the battle of Delium (424 BC), cf. Thucydides iv. 90; and for Socrates' selfless bravery in it, see Plato's *Symposium* 221a–b, *Laches* 181b. The fighting at Amphipolis is probably a battle in 422 BC described in Thucydides v. 2.

29b *life in Hades*: for Hades, see Index of Names. For ignorance of the afterlife, cf. *Phaedo* 66e–67a, 68a–b. See also note on 42a.

29c *I need never have been brought to court . . . death*: Anytus would have preferred Socrates to leave Athens voluntarily, rather than face formal charges. But since Socrates was unwilling to abandon his activities, an indictment was needed. It became necessary for the prosecution to seek the death penalty, in the expectation that the defence would propose exile as an alternative. Socrates here shows that he well understood the plan. Later (37d–38b) he refuses to oblige its proponents. Cf. *Crito* 45e.

30b *It is not wealth . . . public life*: this translation, which is the usual one, makes Socrates utter what some scholars have thought an inappropriate sentiment. Burnet (Bibliography, item 9, 124) remarked that, having stressed the extreme poverty resulting from his service to God (23c, 31b–c), Socrates could 'hardly recommend virtue as a good investment'. Instead, Burnet takes the sentence to mean that only through goodness does wealth or anything else become beneficial to human beings. This idea is developed at *Meno* 87e–89a, *Euthydemus* 279a–281e, *Laws* 661a–d, and in the pseudo-Platonic *Eryxias*. However, Burnet's view, although favoured by several recent writers, places an almost impossible strain upon the Greek. Translated in the usual way, the sentence must mean that goodness is generally (though not always or necessarily) attended by prosperity and other external goods. That position is defended at *Republic* 612b–613e, and by Aristotle (*Politics* 1323a38–b7). Socrates need not be taken to mean that one should seek goodness *in order to* acquire wealth etc. (so he is far from advocating virtue as an 'investment'), but only that those who acquire goodness will normally acquire other benefits as well. Reading the text thus, De Strycker and Slings (Bibliography, item 16, 138–40) aptly compare it with Christ's words in Matthew 6: 33: 'Seek ye first the Kingdom of God and His righteousness, and all these things shall be added unto you.'

30c *abide by my request*: cf. 17c–d.

31b *it would not seem to be in human nature*: Socrates argues that the purely benevolent nature of his mission points to its divine origin. It is not natural for human beings, but only for God, to act solely for the benefit of another. Cf. *Euthyphro* 3d, 15a, and Introduction, p. xiv.

31d *a certain divine or spiritual sign*: Socrates here confirms that his well-known mysterious 'sign' had been used to substantiate the charge of 'introducing new spiritual realities'. Cf. *Euthyphro* 3b with note. At 40b and 41d the *absence* of the sign will be taken as significant. For the implications of this, see Introduction, p. xxiii. Other allusions to the sign in Plato occur at *Euthydemus* 272e, *Republic* 496c, *Theaetetus* 151a, *Phaedrus* 242b–c. A very different account is given by Xenophon in *Memorabilia* i. 1. 1–9, iv. 8. 1–2, and *Defence of Socrates* 12–13. There it is not limited to warnings against Socrates' own intended actions, but enables him to counsel others. See also the pseudo-Platonic *Theages* (128d–131a). Xenophon assimilates the sign to traditional divination, and attributes to Socrates heaven-sent premonitions of events that are unpredictable on the basis of scientific knowledge.

32b *the presiding commission*: fifty representatives from each of the ten tribes who made up the Council (see note on 25a) took turns during the year to provide an executive for the entire body. In this capacity they were called *prutaneis*, and the tribe in office at any given time was said to 'preside' (*prutaneuein*). They met and dined in the 'round chamber' (see 32c with note).

a collective trial . . . the naval battle: in 406 BC, after a sea-battle off the Ionian coast at Arginusae, several Athenian commanders were charged for their failure to rescue the shipwrecked survivors and recover the dead. A motion to try them collectively was endorsed by the Council and referred to the Assembly. Although a collective trial was unconstitutional, the motion was passed by the Assembly after a stormy debate, and six surviving commanders were convicted and executed. The debate, to which Socrates alludes here, is recounted in vivid detail by Xenophon (*Hellenica* i. 7). See Introduction, p. xxxii.

32c *the Thirty*: see Introduction, pp. vii–viii.

the round chamber: a building (*tholos*) also called the 'sun-shade' (*skia*) from its shape. It was commandeered as a seat of government by the Thirty.

Salamis: an island separated by a narrow channel from the coast of Attica.

33a *those whom my slanderers allege to have been my students*: Socrates is probably alluding, especially, to two of his former associates who had become notorious enemies of the Athenian democracy, Alcibiades and Critias. The former was a brilliant but wayward politician, who had turned against Athens and helped her enemies. He plays a major role in Plato's *Symposium* (212d–223a). The latter was an unscrupulous oligarch, who had become a leading member of the Thirty Tyrants. In the light of their subsequent villainous careers, Socrates was widely suspected of having 'corrupted' them. Xenophon (*Memorabilia* i. 2. 24–47) refutes this belief at length. According to him, 'politics had brought them to Socrates, and for politics they left him' (i. 2. 47).

I never . . . was anyone's instructor: Socrates here, in effect, contrasts himself with the sophists, in that he did not set himself up as a professional teacher. See note on 20a and Introduction, p. xix.

33c *through oracles and dreams*: for example, the Delphic oracle, whose answer had led Socrates to undertake his mission. Dreams had long been believed to be a source of divine communication with human beings, and are often so treated by Plato, cf. *Crito*

44a–b, *Phaedo* 60e–61b. See note on 40d, and D. Gallop, *Aristotle on Sleep and Dreams* (Peterborough, 1991), 7–11.

and through every means . . . human being: additional means of divine communication may include direct appearances of gods to human beings, and perhaps also human intelligence, conceived as a god-given faculty. See Introduction, p. xxiii.

34a *Plato here*: Plato's name occurs in his dialogues only here, at 38b below, and at *Phaedo* 59b, where it is noted that he was absent at Socrates' death owing to illness.

34d *in Homer's own words*: the quotation is from *Odyssey*, xix. 163.

my sons: at the time of his trial Socrates had two little boys, Sophroniscus and Menexenus, and an older son, Lamprocles (*Phaedo* 116b).

35b *no better than women*: this is one of many disparaging remarks in Plato about women. Open displays of emotion, especially grief, are regarded as distinctively female, an indulgence of the 'female side' of our nature. Cf. *Phaedo* 60a, 117d–e, *Republic* 387e, 395d, 469d, 605d–e. For Socrates and women, see note on 41c below.

35d *I do acknowledge them . . . as none of my accusers do*: Socrates displays religious faith of an order shared by none of his accusers. For a similar argument in relation to the charges against him, cf. 29a, and see Introduction, p. xxi.

36a *if a mere thirty votes . . . I should have been acquitted*: with a jury of 500, this implies that the vote was 280–220, since at the time of Socrates' trial an evenly split vote (250–250) would have secured his acquittal. Diogenes Laertius (ii. 41) says that Socrates was condemned 'by 281 votes more than those for acquittal'. This cannot be reconciled with the present text. Probably Diogenes, or his source, assumed a jury of 501, and meant that there were 281 votes for condemnation, i.e. 61 more than those for acquittal. Odd-numbered juries are not, however, attested in the first half of the fourth century.

36b *he would not have gained one-fifth of the votes cast*: a minimum proportion of votes was required, on pain of a fine, in order to discourage frivolous prosecutions. Socrates playfully postulates an equal division of the negative votes amongst his three accusers. Each would then be credited with only $93\frac{1}{3}$ votes, i.e. less than one-fifth of the total jury of 500.

what alternative penalty: the court had to decide between the penalty demanded by the prosecution and a counter-penalty proposed by the defence, with no option of substituting a different one. Socrates' accusers would probably have expected him to propose exile. Socrates recognizes that that was what the court would probably have preferred (37c), but refuses to oblige them.

36d *free meals in the Prytaneum*: the Prytaneum was the building on the north-east slope of the Acropolis, in which hospitality was given to honoured guests of the state, and to Olympic victors and other sports-heroes. Hence, in proposing that he be given free meals there, Socrates is asking for treatment normally reserved for persons of outstanding distinction. Moreover, he is brazen enough to propose it in order that he may continue the very activity for which he has just been convicted. The jury had no power to grant such a request, as he well knew. Indeed, he obviously half-expected to be held in contempt of court (37a). His comparison of a philosopher's claim to public recognition with the claims of sports-heroes recalls a poem by Xenophanes. See J. H. Lesher, *Xenophanes of Colophon* (Toronto, 1992), 55–61, 74.

37a *I do not treat any human being unjustly, at least intentionally*: cf. 26a with note.

as in other jurisdictions . . . over several: this was the law at Sparta, because of the irrevocability of capital punishment. In the *Laws* (855c–856a) Plato proposes a legal procedure requiring capital cases to be tried over three consecutive days.

37b *I don't know if that is a good thing or a bad one*: cf. 29a–b.

37c *the annually appointed prison commissioners*: literally, 'the Eleven', a commission responsible for prisons and state executions.

37e *if I repel them . . . will expel me on their account*: it is not clear (*a*) why young people in other cities should get rid of Socrates by putting pressure on their parents, if his ideas repel them, or (*b*) why he should expect such a different reception from the one he had enjoyed from the youth of Athens. On the other hand, if he does not repel them, it is not obvious why their elders should regard him less favourably than the relatives whom he had named as supporters at 33d–34a. Perhaps he had reason to believe that other communities would be less tolerant than Athens of free intellectual inquiry.

38a *you will . . . think that I am practising a sly evasion*: Socrates refers to his 'irony' (*eirōneia*), a charge made by his enemies, and often interpreted as an insincere disavowal of knowledge. For its supposed relevance to the *Euthyphro*, see Introduction, p. xv. Although its role is different in the present passage, the notion of insincerity is still present. The jury will imagine that Socrates is invoking God's will only as a pretext for refusing to give up philosophy.

an unexamined life is no life for a human being to live: the most celebrated line in the *Defence*. Note that Socrates' examination of others is inseparable from examination of himself (cf. 28e). 'Examining' therefore includes 'being examined'. Its importance for a worthwhile *human* life reminds us of the removal of the false conceit of knowledge, which Socrates had earlier (20d) called 'a *human* kind of wisdom'. See notes on 23a, 23b, and Introduction, p. xx.

38b *30 minas*: this seems to have been a normal amount for a fine, and was a considerable sum. See note on 20b. According to Xenophon, however, Socrates refused to propose any fine, or allow his friends to do so, on the ground that that would have been an admission of guilt (*Defence of Socrates* 23).

38d *those who condemned me to death*: Diogenes Laertius (ii. 42) says that the death sentence was passed with an accession of eighty fresh votes. If so, the vote would have been 360–140. See note on 36a.

do or say anything: this phrase, repeated at 39a, also occurs in the argument of *Euthyphro* 8c–d, that no one will be so shameless as to admit wrongdoing, yet try to escape punishment. Here Socrates uses it to make the point that he was not willing to pay any price to secure acquittal.

39b *fleeter of foot than death*: literally, 'runs faster than death'. The Greek words form an alliterative jingle, which may have been proverbial.

as judged by Truth: for the personification of 'truth', cf. *Crito* 48a, *Symposium* 201c, *Phaedo* 91c, *Republic* 597e.

39c *when they are on the point of death*: for prophecy when death is imminent, cf. Socrates' comparison of himself with the prophetic swans of Apollo in the *Phaedo* (85a–b).

as soon as I am dead retribution will come upon you: this section has an aggressive, almost vengeful tone, in curious contrast with the forgiving spirit of 41d. Socrates' 'avengers' may be the youthful disciples who had used his methods of cross-examination upon others (23c). But there is no evidence that such activities intensified after his death. According to Diogenes Laertius (ii. 106, iii. 6), Plato and other disciples swiftly betook themselves to Megara.

40a *in applying that term to you, I probably use it correctly*: only at this point does Socrates begin to address (some of) his jurors as 'gentlemen of the jury'. See note on 17a. Those who voted against him are not 'judges', properly speaking, because they have failed to judge him according to the principles they were sworn to observe (35c–d, cf. 18a).

40d *the kind in which the sleeper does not even dream at all*: literally 'does not even see a dream'. In Greek idiom, dreams are always 'seen', a usage which reflects the archaic view of the dream as a figure experienced in a distinctive mode of vision. See note on 33c, and E. R. Dodds, *The Greeks and the Irrational* (Berkeley, 1951), 104–6.

40e *the Great King of Persia*: this monarch embodied the popular ideal of happiness (cf. *Gorgias* 470e, *Euthydemus* 274a). Socrates does not claim that a night of dreamless sleep is 'happy', but only that very few days or nights in anyone's life, even the Great King's, are spent 'better and more agreeably' (40d). He expects happiness or 'good fortune' (*eudaimonia*) only on his alternative hypothesis, an afterlife in which he can meet and cross-examine heroes of the past (41c).

41a *who are also said to sit in judgment there*: for the judges see Index of Names, s.vv. Aeacus, Minos, Rhadamanthys, Triptolemus. It is not clear whether Socrates envisages them merely as judging disputes among the dead, or as passing judgment upon the earthly life of those who enter Hades. If the latter, he may be thinking of an 'appeal' in the next world against his unjust treatment in this one. Just such an idea is elaborated by Plato in the closing myth of the *Gorgias* (523a–527a).

41c *the leader of the great expedition against Troy*: Agamemnon, chief of the Greek forces in the Trojan War. Cf. 28c with note.

countless other men and women: at *Symposium* 215d Socrates' audience is said to include women, and the same dialogue features his own encounter with Diotima, a wise woman from Mantinea. In the present passage he probably imagines himself examining wise women of bygone ages, or mythical figures such as Diotima. The whole passage seems to be inspired by the visit of Odysseus to the underworld in Homer's *Odyssey*, Book xi, and his encounters with the souls of the dead.

41d *better I should die now and be rid of my troubles*: by his 'troubles', Socrates probably means the infirmities of old age. A wish to escape these was, according to Xenophon, what motivated his conduct at his trial. Contrast, however, what Plato makes him say at 19a, and see Introduction, pp. xvi–xvii.

41e *this much I ask of them*: it would be odd if Socrates meant to restrict his final request to the jurors who had voted against him. Also surprising, given what he had said of them at 39b–d, is the suggestion that, if his sons are properly admonished, he will have received his 'just deserts' from them. It seems better to take his final request as intended for the whole jury.

42a *unclear to everyone, save only to God*: Socrates' closing words show him to be free from the false conceit of knowledge (cf. 21d, 23b), specifically knowledge about death (cf. 29a–b). They express a serene faith in God, which also marks the end of the *Crito*. See notes on 20e and *Crito* 54e.

CRITO

43c *the ship has come back from Delos*: the small island of Delos was sacred to the god Apollo. A mission sailed there annually from Athens to commemorate her deliverance by Theseus from servitude to King Minos of Crete. No executions could be carried out in Athens until the sacred ship returned (*Phaedo* 58b–c).

43d *Sunium*: the headland at the south-eastern extremity of Attica, about 50 kilometres from Athens. The winds were unfavourable at the time (*Phaedo* 58c), so the ship may have been taking shelter at Sunium when the travellers left it there.

44a *a certain dream I had in the night*: see notes on *Defence* 33c, 40d.

44b *Thou shalt . . . third day*: in Homer's *Iliad* (ix. 363) Achilles says, 'on the third day I may return to fertile Phthia', meaning that he can get home in three days. In Socrates' dream 'Phthia' becomes a symbol for the 'home' to which he will return after his death.

44d *they are unable to give anyone understanding or lack of it*: the implication, that understanding and ignorance are the greatest good and the worst of evils, is Socrates' constant theme in the *Defence*. See Introduction, p. xx. For the translation 'understanding', see note on *Defence* 18b.

44e *the blackmailers*: Athens had no public prosecutors. Pro-secutions were undertaken by private citizens, who sometimes threatened legal action for personal, political, or financial gain. The word *sukophantēs* means, literally, 'one who shows figs'. It is uncertain how it acquired its legal sense. One theory con-nects it with revealing the fruit on a fig-tree by shaking the tree, hence extorting money by accusation or blackmail. The sense of 'toady', borne by its modern derivative 'sycophant', was not present in the Greek word.

45b *as you were saying in court*: cf. *Defence* 37c–d.

45c *Thessaly*: the region of northern Greece, lying 200–300 kilo-metres north-west of Attica. According to Diogenes Laertius (ii. 25) Socrates refused invitations from residents of Crannon and Larissa, two cities in Thessaly.

those sons of yours: see note on *Defence* 34d.

45d *if one professes to cultivate goodness*: a palpable hit at Soc-rates, who has professed to care for nothing else. The blow will be effectively parried, however, at 51a and 53c. See Introduc-tion, pp. xxxi–xxxii.

45e *when that could have been avoided*: see *Defence* 29c with note.

46b *to follow nothing within me but the principle*: the word trans-lated 'principle' (*logos*) can also mean 'argument', and is some-times so rendered here. But in what follows Socrates seems to be thinking of principles that must guide his conduct, rather than the arguments by which those principles had been estab-lished. By calling a principle something 'within him', Socrates virtually personifies it as a force motivating his actions.

46c *more bogeymen*: Socrates compares death and other terrors with bogeys used to frighten children. Cf. *Phaedo* 77d–e. He will also distinguish serious, adult argument from childish non-sense (46d, 49b). The 'bogeys' mentioned are all standard in-struments of law enforcement. For the implication of this, see Introduction, p. xxxiii.

47a *how were such points established?*: this evidently refers to dis-cussions held between Socrates and Crito on previous occasions (cf. 46c–d, 48b, 49a–b). The method of establishing the point is argument by analogy, a favourite Socratic technique. See also next note.

47b *not those of most people*: this passage recalls the arguments of *Defence* 20a–c, 25a–c, that only one person, or very few, can possess expertise in any given field, whereas the majority are ignorant. It also anticipates the important argument of the *Theaetetus* (152a–179d), which attacks the thesis that all truth is subjective, and that one man's opinion is as true as another's.

47d *assuming that some expert exists*: the idea that there is an expert in moral matters, comparable with the doctor in health matters, is fundamental to all of Plato's ethical and political thought. Such expertise is the province of the philosopher, and is the aim of all Socratic inquiry. The role of the moral expert affects the way in which the arguments of the *Crito* are structured. See note on 49b, and Introduction, p. xxvi.

the element which . . . is made better by what is just, but is spoilt by what is unjust: this element is what is referred to in the *Defence* (29e), and often elsewhere, as the 'soul' (*psuchē*), that precious part of human beings whose good condition constitutes their true well-being, and must therefore be of paramount concern. Here, as often in Plato, the effect of wrongdoing upon the soul is compared with the effect of unhealthy practices upon the body. Cf. *Republic* 444c–445b.

48a *Truth*: see note on *Defence* 39b.

48b *living well is the same as living honourably or justly*: this equation puts Plato's ethical theory in a nutshell. A full defence of it is not undertaken in the *Crito*. See Introduction, p. xxi.

49b *one should not return injustice*: this clearly follows from the general principle that one should not act unjustly in any circumstances whatever. It is because the principle, and particularly the inference drawn from it here, would be widely denied, that Socrates has argued for trusting the moral expert rather than majority opinion. See Introduction, p. xxvi.

49d *contrary to your real beliefs*: Socrates often insists that his respondents answer according to their real beliefs. Where they fail or refuse to do so, discussion proves futile, because—as he says here—they share 'no common counsel', i.e. no basis for joint deliberation.

49e *provided they are just*: for the interpretation of this important proviso, and its role in the argument, see Introduction, p. xxviii.

50a *would we be abiding by the things we agreed*: the notion of an agreement between the citizen and the state is often said to prefigure the 'Social Contract' theory of political obligation, according to which the individual surrenders some degree of personal liberty in return for benefits from the state. Note, however, that the agreement is here made between the individual and the state, not between individuals and one another. In this respect the present theory differs from the version of the 'Social Contract' put forward at *Republic* 358e–359b.

or whatever else one should call it: it is implied that any other word would be a mere euphemism for 'running away', a term of contempt for deserting soldiers or runaway slaves. Cf. 52d, 53d. Fleeing in battle is treated by Socrates as a paradigm of cowardice (*Defence* 28e, 39a). In the *Phaedo* (62b) deserting one's post provides an analogy for committing suicide, as it does here for breaking gaol. All of these acts involve disobedience to higher authority: military commanders, courts of law, or God.

50b *With this action you are attempting, do you intend anything short of destroying us . . .?*: in raising this question, the Laws are often thought to be using a generalizing argument of the form 'what would happen if everyone were to break the law?' since only on that hypothesis would the laws and the state be 'destroyed'. No such argument, however, need be read into the text. See Introduction, p. xxx.

particularly a legal advocate: it was customary in Athens to appoint a public advocate to defend laws which it was proposed to abrogate. By alluding to this procedure, the Laws perhaps insinuate the absurdity of 'abrogating' the fundamental principle that they go on to mention. See next note.

the one requiring that judgments, once rendered, shall have authority: these words have been read as referring to a specific law passed when the Athenian democracy was restored after the fall of the Thirty Tyrants in 403 (Burnet (Bibliography, item 9), 201). It had reinstated judgments made by the democratic courts before the regime of the Thirty. But it would be pointless to invoke a law framed specifically to uphold judgments made five years before Socrates' own trial. The Laws are better understood as invoking a basic general principle upon which any legal system must depend. See Introduction, pp. xxix–xxx.

50c *question-and-answer*: the Laws allude to Socrates' much-vaunted preference for this method, to which he had referred in the *Defence* (e.g. 17c, 27b, 33b, 41c).

50e *in the arts and physical training*: the standard components of traditional Athenian education, in terms of which Plato discusses education in the *Republic*, Books ii–iii.

51b *you should revere your fatherland, deferring to it and appeasing it when it is angry*: in a cascade of patriotic rhetoric, the Laws here demand a degree of subservience that has often been found offensive. Indeed, their talk of 'appeasement' suggests precisely the kind of grovelling behaviour with which Socrates had refused to demean himself in court (*Defence* 34d–35b). Although he is made to raise no objection to their present speech, we need not suppose that Plato would have endorsed every word of it, or meant his readers to do so. The Laws speak only from their own point of view. See Introduction, p. xxxiii.

You must either persuade it, or else do whatever it commands: the Laws claim that the city remains open to persuasion, an important point repeated twice below (51b–c, 51e–52a). They do not, however, say explicitly how Socrates might have 'persuaded' the city, or identify the 'command' relevant to his case. The 'command' is, presumably, the death sentence passed upon him. Since he had failed to 'persuade' the jury to acquit him or to substitute an alternative penalty, it is that command which, according to the Laws, he is now obliged to obey.

being beaten or put in bonds . . . to be wounded or killed: it is notable that all the examples in this passage are of things that the obedient citizen must *suffer*, not of things that he must *do*. For the significance of this point, see Introduction, p. xxviii.

you must neither give way nor retreat, nor leave your position: once again, the Laws use military metaphors for dereliction of duty. See note on 50a.

51c *or else persuade it as to what is truly just*: the language hints at a conception of 'natural' justice which transcends the dictates of the law. Socrates must obey the city's commands, unless he can persuade it that he has *moral* right on his side.

against your fatherland: the analogy between doing violence to one's country and doing it to one's parents has been subtly reinforced, throughout this speech, by the fact that the word often translated 'country' (*patris*) is cognate with 'father' (*patēr*).

51d *once he has been admitted to adult status*: admission to Athenian citizenship was not automatic, but required formal registration by males at the age of 17 or 18, with proof of age and parental citizenship. The procedure is described, and its implications for the argument of the Laws well discussed, by Kraut (Bibliography, item 20), 154–7.

may . . . go wherever he pleases: this line of argument would not be available to any state which controls its borders by means of passports.

52b *more than is normal for all other Athenians*: Phaedrus, in the Platonic dialogue named after him (230c–d), remarks that Socrates never so much as sets foot outside the city walls. Socrates replies that he is a lover of learning, and cannot learn anything from the trees and open country, as he can from people in town.

except once to go to the Isthmus: the Isthmus was the strip of land linking the Peloponnese with the rest of Greece. Socrates may have attended the Isthmian Games, which were held every two years at Corinth.

52c *you would choose death ahead of exile, so you said*: cf. *Defence* 37c–d.

52d *trying to run away*: see note on 50a.

52e *seventy years*: an exaggeration. Socrates was only 70 at the time of his trial (*Defence* 17d). He could hardly have had the option of leaving Athens for another city before he came of age.

neither Lacedaemon nor Crete: Lacedaemon was the official name for the territory of Sparta. Sparta and Crete were both authoritarian and 'closed' societies, which forbade their citizens to live abroad. Plato's attitude towards them is not uncritical. Accounts of the Spartan way of life occur at *Hippias Major* 283a–286a and *Protagoras* 342a–343c, both heavily spiced with irony. In the latter passage Crete is conjoined with Sparta, and speakers from both states appear in Plato's *Laws*, which is set in Crete. For comparison of their political systems with that of Athens, see Kraut (Bibliography, item 20), 177–80, 215–28.

53b *Thebes or Megara*: Thebes was the chief city in Boeotia, the region lying to the north-west of Attica; Megara was on the Isthmus (see note on 52b). Both lay within easy reach of Athens.

a subverter of laws: in support of this claim, see Introduction, p. xxx.

53d *Thessaly*: see note on 45c.

54a *Hades*: see Index of Names.

54c *treated unjustly not by us Laws, but by human beings*: for an explanation of this highly questionable distinction, see Introduction, p. xxxi. The Laws never concede that they have wronged

Socrates. They had thought it just to destroy him (51a), and remain unpersuaded that they have done anything amiss (51e).

54d *the Corybantic revellers*: the Corybantes performed orgiastic rites and dances to the sound of pipe and drum music. Their music sometimes induced a state of frenzy in emotionally disordered people, which was followed by a deep sleep from which the patients awoke cured. Socrates compares the arguments of the Laws with Corybantic music, which continues to ring in the ears even when the instruments have ceased to play.

54e *God*: or 'the god'. Socrates may be referring to his own guiding deity; but a deeper, monotheistic note seems audible in his final words, as also at the close of the *Defence*. See note on *Defence* 42a.

TEXTUAL NOTES

I have translated the Greek of the revised Oxford Classical Text, ed.
W. S. M. Nicoll *et al.*, *Platonis Opera*, vol. i (Oxford University
Press, 1995), except in the following places, indicated in the trans-
lations by an obelisk (†). Line references are to the revised OCT. The
MS readings mentioned are derived from its critical apparatus.

EUTHYPHRO

4b1 Omitting ὀρθῶς (Burnet).
5d4 Omitting κατὰ τὴν ἀνοσιότητα (Hutchinson).
10d10 Reading καὶ θεοφιλὲς ⟨τὸ θεοφιλές⟩ (Bast). For defence of
  this emendation, see Cohen in Bibliography, item 38, pp. 169–70
  n. 19.
12b1 Reading οὐκ ἐθέλεις νεικεῖν (Hutchinson).

DEFENCE OF SOCRATES

17a6 Reading χρῆ with some MSS.
23c2 Reading μοι ⟨οἱ⟩ ἐπακολουθοῦντες (De Strycker and Slings).
27e2 Omitting ἢ (Forster).
27e4–5 Omitting τὴν γραφὴν ταύτην as a gloss on ταῦτα (De
  Strycker and Slings).
27e7 Reading οὐ τοῦ αὐτοῦ with some MSS.
29b1 Reading καίτοι with Eusebius.
31d7 Omitting πάλαι (Cobet).
32b4 Reading ἐβούλεσθε with some MSS.
35b4 Reading ἡμᾶς with V and the Armenian translation.
36d7 Omitting οὕτως (Adam).

CRITO

43d4–5 Omitting τῶν ἀγγέλων (Hirschig).

INDEX OF NAMES

Adimantus: older brother of Plato, mentioned as present at Socrates' trial (*Defence* 34a). He and Plato's other brother, Glaucon, are Socrates' main interlocutors in the *Republic*, Books ii–x.

Aeacus: one of the three judges in Hades, mentioned at *Defence* 41a and in the myth of the afterlife in the *Gorgias* (523e, 526c). He also appears as a judge and lawgiver of the island Aegina, and an arbiter of disputes among the gods.

Aeantodorus: brother of APOLLODORUS, mentioned at *Defence* 34a, but otherwise unknown.

Aeschines: devotee of Socrates, who wrote speeches for the lawcourts, taught oratory, and was admired as an author of Socratic dialogues. A few fragments of his writings are extant. He was present at Socrates' trial (*Defence* 33e) and death (*Phaedo* 59b).

Ajax: Greek hero of the Trojan War, mentioned at *Defence* 41b as a victim of an 'unjust verdict'. This refers to the award of Achilles' armour to ODYSSEUS in a contest with Ajax. The latter's resulting madness and suicide are the subject of *Ajax*, one of the extant tragedies by Sophocles.

Anaxagoras: Presocratic philosopher, originally from Clazomenae in Ionia. Important fragments of his work are extant. He spent many years in Athens and was prominent in Athenian intellectual life, as the reference to his doctrines (*Defence* 26d) suggests. His philosophical views, especially his explanation of the physical world as due to 'intelligence', are scathingly criticized at *Phaedo* 97c–99c.

Antiphon: from Cephisia, father of EPIGENES and supporter of Socrates at his trial (*Defence* 33e), but not otherwise known.

Anytus: leading Athenian democratic politician and accuser of Socrates, and the main instigator of the prosecution. He appears briefly in Plato's *Meno* (89e–95a), where he displays a threatening attitude towards Socrates and intense hostility to the sophists. Stories in Xenophon, *Defence of Socrates* 29–31, suggest personal antipathy between him and Socrates.

Apollodorus: ardent devotee of Socrates, notorious for his emotional volatility (*Phaedo* 59b, 117d). He was one of the friends who offered to guarantee a fine for Socrates (*Defence* 38b). He is also the narrator of Plato's *Symposium*, where he is portrayed as a fanatical convert to philosophy (173d).

Ariston: Athenian of distinguished lineage, and father of Plato.

Aristophanes: c.450–385. The most famous playwright of Athenian Old Comedy. Eleven of his plays and many fragments are extant. He also appears as a principal character in Plato's *Symposium* (189a–193d).

Callias: wealthy Athenian patron of sophistic culture. His house is the scene of Plato's *Protagoras* and Xenophon's *Symposium*.

Cebes: citizen of Thebes in Boeotia, who had studied there with the Pythagorean philosopher Philolaus. A disciple of Socrates, he and SIMMIAS are Socrates' main interlocutors in the *Phaedo*. Xenophon mentions them both, along with other associates of Socrates, as admirable men (*Memorabilia* i. 2. 48).

Chaerephon: long-time faithful follower of Socrates. Expelled from Athens in 404 during the regime of the Thirty Tyrants, he returned when the democracy was restored in the following year. Plato (*Defence* 21a) and Xenophon (*Defence of Socrates* 14) both make him the questioner who asked the Delphic oracle whether any man was wiser than Socrates. He also appears briefly at the start of Plato's *Gorgias* and *Charmides*, and has a role in ARISTOPHANES' *Clouds*. The comic poets nicknamed him 'the bat' from his squeaky voice.

Crito: Socrates' contemporary, fellow demesman, and one of his closest friends. He is Socrates' interlocutor in the dialogue named after him, plays an important role in the dramatic action of the *Phaedo* (63d–e, 115b–118a), and appears in the prologue and epilogue of the *Euthydemus*.

Critobulus: son of CRITO and member of the Socratic circle, who was present at Socrates' trial and death (*Defence* 33e, *Phaedo* 59b). He is criticized by Socrates in Xenophon's *Memorabilia* i. 3. 8–10 for kissing a pretty boy. In Xenophon's *Symposium*, his own beauty and amorous susceptibility are subjects of light-hearted sexual banter (4. 10–28, 5. 1–10).

Cronus: mythical son of URANUS (Heaven) and Gaea (Earth), father of ZEUS, and his predecessor as chief among the gods. He mutilated his father, married his sister Rhea, and devoured his children, except for Zeus, who overthrew him. These stories are told in HESIOD's *Theogony* (154–210, 453–506).

Daedalus: legendary artist, craftsman, and inventor. His many marvellous works included the labyrinth for the Minotaur in the palace of King Minos of Crete, and wings for himself and his son, Icarus. He was also believed to have made statues that could open their eyes, walk, and move their arms.

Demodocus: father of THEAGES, and a character in the pseudo-Platonic *Theages*, where he is said (127d–e) to be older than Socrates and to have held many of the highest offices in Athens. He may be the general of the same name mentioned by Thucydides (iv. 75) for the year 425–4. The spurious works in the Platonic corpus include a dialogue bearing his name.

Epigenes: an associate of Socrates. Xenophon records a conversation between them (*Memorabilia* iii. 12) in which Socrates advised him to take more exercise. He was present at Socrates' death (*Phaedo* 59b).

Euthyphro: self-proclaimed expert on religious law, and Socrates' interlocutor in the dialogue named after him. Since Plato portrays him as somewhat eccentric, it is a nice irony that his name should mean 'Straight-Thinker' or 'Right-Mind'. See Introduction, p. ix.

Evenus: a professional teacher of human excellence, or 'sophist'. In the *Defence* (20b–c) and *Phaedo* (60d, 61b–c) he is mentioned with obvious irony. It is hinted that he is concerned only with worldly success, and is therefore not a genuine philosopher in the Socratic sense.

Gorgias: *c.*480–376, from Leontini in Sicily; commonly but perhaps wrongly classified as a 'sophist'. He cultivated an artificial but influential prose style, and gave lessons in rhetoric, or effective public speaking. He plays a significant part in the powerful dialogue named after him, in which Plato explores the dangers of rhetoric.

Hades: the underworld inhabited by the dead. The name belongs, properly, to the mythical king of that realm, who was the brother of ZEUS and Poseidon.

Hector: son of Priam, and leading Trojan hero in the war between Greece and Troy. In HOMER's *Iliad* he kills PATROCLUS, squire of Achilles, who in turn avenges his friend's death by slaying Hector.

Hephaestus: lame god of fire and of the forge, and associated with volcanoes in Greek mythology. He was cast out of heaven by his mother HERA because he was deformed (*Iliad* xviii. 393–7). In revenge he sent her a golden throne to which she was chained with invisible bonds when she sat upon it.

Hera: daughter of CRONUS, wife and sister of ZEUS, and mother of HEPHAESTUS.

Hesiod: one of the earliest extant Greek poets. His *Theogony* contains an account of the origin of the traditional gods. His *Works and Days* is a didactic poem giving moral and practical precepts about rural life.

Hippias: itinerant teacher or 'sophist', probably a close contemporary of Socrates, who claimed expertise in many subjects. Two dialogues in the Platonic corpus bearing his name portray him as a polymath filled with conceit at his own learning. Comical impressions of him are given in Plato's *Protagoras* (315c, 337c–338a).

Hipponicus: member of wealthy Athenian family, and father of CALLIAS.

Homer: greatest epic poet of Greece, and composer of the *Iliad* and the *Odyssey*. The *Iliad* contains episodes from the legendary Trojan War, while the *Odyssey* recounts the travels and adventures of the hero ODYSSEUS during his journey home after the war.

Leon: resident of Salamis, unjustly arrested and murdered by the Thirty Tyrants in 404. The episode is attested by Plato (*Defence* 32c–d) and Xenophon (*Hellenica* ii. 3. 39, *Memorabilia* iv. 4. 3), and in Plato's Seventh Letter (324d–325a).

Lycon: Athenian politician and co-accuser of Socrates with MELETUS and ANYTUS. Apart from references to him in the *Defence* (23e–24a, 36a), he remains a shadowy figure.

Lysanias: of Sphettus, father of AESCHINES. Mentioned in the *Defence* (33e) but otherwise unknown.

Meletus: youthful co-accuser of Socrates with ANYTUS and LYCON. He drew up the indictment against Socrates, but was evidently a mere tool of Anytus. A poet named 'Meletus' is satirized by ARISTOPHANES in the *Frogs* (1302). Since our Meletus is said to have been aggrieved on behalf of the poets (*Defence* 23e), he may have been that poet's son. 'Meletus' is also the name of the prosecutor in the notorious impiety trial of Andocides, which occurred in the same year as that of Socrates. These prosecutors may have been one and the same Meletus. If so, he would appear to have been a religious fanatic, whose zeal served the political purposes of Anytus. Meletus, although not mentioned at *Defence* 32c–d, may also have been one of those directed by the Thirty Tyrants to fetch LEON of Salamis for execution. See Burnet (Bibliography, item 9), 9–10, and De Strycker and Slings (Bibliography, item 16), 94–5.

Minos: legendary king of Crete, and traditional judge in the underworld. He is mentioned with AEACUS and RHADAMANTHYS at *Defence* 41a and *Gorgias* 523e, and in HOMER's *Odyssey* (xi. 568–71) as judging disputes among the dead. A dialogue bearing his name is among the spurious works in the Platonic corpus.

Musaeus: mythical bard or singer, closely connected with ORPHEUS. Plato couples them at *Defence* 41a, *Protagoras* 316d, *Republic* 364e.

Nicostratus: supporter of Socrates, present at his trial (*Defence* 33e) but otherwise unknown.

Odysseus: legendary hero in HOMER's *Iliad*, and central figure in the *Odyssey*, which recounts his wanderings after the Trojan War.

Orpheus: legendary bard and founder of the archaic mystical or religious movement known as 'Orphism'. While Orphic ideas about the afterlife are sometimes echoed in Plato, Socrates' hope of meeting Orpheus in the next world (*Defence* 41a) need not be taken to imply any special interest in those ideas. He is mentioned along with MUSAEUS, HOMER, and HESIOD simply as a renowned ancestor of poetic tradition.

Palamedes: Greek hero of the Trojan War, credited with invention of the alphabet. In one tradition he was a rival of ODYSSEUS, who fabricated evidence to get him unjustly convicted and stoned to death on charges of treason. Socrates compares his own unjust conviction with that of Palamedes in both Xenophon's *Defence of Socrates* (26) and Plato's (41b).

Paralius: supporter of Socrates who was present at his trial (*Defence* 33e), but is not otherwise known. His brother was THEAGES.

Patroclus: squire and close friend of Achilles in HOMER's *Iliad*, slain by HECTOR and avenged by Achilles.

Prodicus: itinerant teacher from Ceos, and one of the sophists prominent in Plato's *Protagoras*, where he is comically described (315d–316a) and his love of drawing fine distinctions between close synonyms is parodied (337a–c). In the *Cratylus* (384b) Socrates claims to have been his student.

Proteus: mythical 'old man of the sea', who eluded all attempts at capture by constantly changing his form. He appears in HOMER's *Odyssey* iv. 382–570.

Rhadamanthys: with AEACUS and MINOS one of the three traditional judges in the underworld; mentioned also in the *Gorgias* (523e) and *Laws* (625a, 948b–c) as conspicuous for his justice.

Simmias: citizen of Thebes and follower of Socrates, who was prepared to finance his escape from gaol (*Crito* 45b). He and CEBES are Socrates' main interlocutors in the *Phaedo*.

Sisyphus: mythical wrongdoer, called 'craftiest of men' by HOMER (*Iliad* vi. 153), and famous for his endless punishment in the underworld. His task was to push a boulder up to the top of a hill, from which it always rolled down again (*Odyssey* xi. 593–600). A dialogue bearing his name appears among the spurious works in the Platonic corpus.

Tantalus: mythical king of Phrygia, possessing proverbial wealth. In one tradition he tried to make himself immortal by stealing the food of the gods. For this he was punished by being made to stand in water which receded as soon as he stooped to drink, and to stretch out for fruit which the wind always blew away from his grasp. See *Odyssey*, xi. 582–92.

Telamon: legendary king of Salamis and father of AJAX.

Theages: disciple of Socrates, whose brother PARALIUS was present at the trial, though Theages himself was already dead (*Defence* 34a). In the *Republic* (496b–c) he is spoken of as one who had been saved for philosophy by the 'bridle' of ill health. A dialogue featuring him and bearing his name is among the spurious works in the Platonic corpus.

Theodotus: associate of Socrates who died before his trial (*Defence* 33e), but is not otherwise known.

Theozotides: father of NICOSTRATUS and THEODOTUS. Though deceased by the time of Socrates' trial, he is known to have introduced two important democratic measures after the fall of the Thirty Tyrants. Plato may therefore have mentioned him in the *Defence* (33e) to counter suspicion that Socrates had anti-democratic leanings. See De Strycker and Slings (Bibliography, item 16), 174–5.

Thetis: sea-nymph or goddess, given in marriage to the mortal Peleus. Achilles was her only child.

Triptolemus: mythical agricultural hero from Eleusis, and a central figure in its mystery cults. Only in the *Defence* (41a), where he is associated with judges in the underworld, does he have any judicial function.

Uranus: heaven or the sky, conceived in mythology as child and husband of Gaea (earth). Chief deity before his son CRONUS.

Zeus: son of CRONUS, and chief among the Olympian gods.

GENERAL INDEX

Figures in **bold type** refer to the text of the *Euthyphro, Defence of Socrates,* or *Crito.* Square brackets indicate Platonic dialogues believed to be spurious.

The Oxford World's Classics Website

www.worldsclassics.co.uk

- Browse the full range of Oxford World's Classics online

- Sign up for our monthly e-alert to receive information on new titles

- Read extracts from the Introductions

- Listen to our editors and translators talk about the world's greatest literature with our Oxford World's Classics audio guides

- Join the conversation, follow us on Twitter at OWC_Oxford

- Teachers and lecturers can order inspection copies quickly and simply via our website

www.worldsclassics.co.uk